JANE'S
NAVAL REVIEW

edited by Captain John Moore RN

JANE'S NAVAL REVIEW

edited by Captain John Moore RN

Fourth year of issue

JANE'S

Copyright © Jane's Publishing Ltd 1985

First published in the United Kingdom in 1985 by
Jane's Publishing Company Limited
238 City Road, London EC1V 2PU

Distributed in the Philippines and the
USA and its dependencies by
Jane's Publishing Inc
135 West 50th Street
New York, NY 10020

ISBN 0 7106 0335 5

Printed in the United Kingdom by
Biddles Ltd, Guildford, Surrey

Contents

The Contributors

Armstrong, Dr Terence

Dr Armstrong is based at the Scott Polar Research Institute and is a contributor to *Polar Record*.

Bildt, Carl

Member of the Swedish Parliament and defence spokesman for the main opposition party.

Crowe, Admiral William J., USN

Commissioned into the US Navy in 1947, Adm Crowe entered the Naval Submarine School in 1948 and subsequently commanded USS *Trout* and Submarine Division 31. Shore assignments before his promotion to Flag rank included Administrative Assistant to the Deputy of Naval Operations (Plans and Policy), and Director of the East Asia and Pacific Branch, Politico-Military Division, Office of the Chief of Naval Operations. Appointed Admiral in March 1980, he assumed his present responsibilities as C-in-C US Pacific Command in July 1983.

Ebata, Kensuke

Born five years after the end of the Second World War, he is one of the most objective and respected of Japanese defence writers. Educated in Tokyo, he graduated in mechanical engineering.

Eberle, Admiral Sir James

During the Second World War and subsequently he served in all sizes of surface ship, from MTBs to an aircraft carrier. Later appointments included Flag Officer Sea Training, Flag Officer Aircraft Carriers and Amphibious Ships, Chief of Fleet Support, C-in-C Fleet, and C-in-C Naval Home Command. Became director of the Royal Institute of International Affairs in January 1984.

Grazebrook, A. W.

Joined RNR in October 1952 and transferred to RANR in 1963. Author of numerous articles in *Pacific Defence Reporter*. Adviser to *Jane's Fighting Ships*.

Lachamade, Pierre

Pen name of a well known French naval officer whose career has taken him to many of the parts of the world currently covered by the French Navy.

Lewin, Admiral of the Fleet Lord, KG, GCB, MVO, DSC

First served in the Admiralty as a commander some 30 years ago. After a spell at sea he returned as deputy director of the staff division responsible for the Royal Navy's tactical, ship and weapon policy. To sea again in command of a frigate squadron, he returned as director of the same division. Command of the carrier HMS *Hermes* was followed by another spell in the Ministry of Defence as Assistant Chief of Naval Staff for Policy. A final period afloat as the seagoing Second-in-Command of the Far East Fleet preceded three years as Vice-Chief of Naval Staff. Subsequent appointments were C-in-C Fleet, combined with the major NATO commands of C-in-C Channel and Eastern Atlantic; C-in-C Naval Home Command; Chief of Naval Staff; and Chief of Defence Staff. This last appointment coincided with the Falklands War.

Ling, Nigel, TEng(CEI)

Served as a Merchant Navy engineer officer, worked on research and development of fishing vessels, including stability investigations, and is currently with the British Transport Docks Board, concerned with naval architecture and design.

Moore, Captain J. E., RN

Entered RN 1939. Served most of naval career in HM Submarines. Commanded 7th Submarine Squadron, was Chief of Staff to Commander-in-Chief Naval Home Command and, finally, took charge of Soviet naval intelligence in MoD. Retired at own request 1972. Editor *Janes Fighting Ships* since November 1972. Author of several books and numbers of articles on naval affairs.

Morison, Samuel L.

Grandson of Professor Samuel Eliot Morison, famous maritime historian and US Naval Historian for Second World War. Author of several books and articles, including *Ships and Aircraft of the US Fleet* and, with John Rowe, *Warships of the US Navy*.

Ronneberg, Commodore Harald, RNN

Served during and after the Second World War in

submarines, completing his naval career in command of that branch of the Royal Norwegian Navy. Has since acted as defence correspondent for several Norwegian newspaper and as editor of service periodicals.

Scheina, Dr Robert L.

After service with US Naval Intelligence became official historian to the US Coast Guard. Author of many articles. Expert on South American naval history. Technical consultant to *Jane's Fighting Ships*.

Suvorov, Victor

After several years on the planning staff of Soviet Military Intelligence (GRV) he emigrated with his family to the West. Author of a number of highly detailed analyses of Soviet military thinking and capability.

Introduction

One of the more misleading modern platitudes holds that air travel has caused the world to shrink. This may be true for those flying from London to Australia or from New York to Hawaii, but it takes no account of the fact that 98 per cent of the world's trade is carried by sea. The average speed of merchant ships has certainly increased over the past 40 years, but it still takes a 20kt ship over 11 days to travel from San Francisco via Hawaii to Tokyo, and 13½ days to go from Melbourne to Aden. Some Britons became temporarily aware of these huge distances when, in 1982, the newspapers discovered that the Operation Corporate task force had to steam 8,000 miles from Portsmouth to the Falklands, taking nearly 11 days at an average speed of 20kt.

Many people are inclined to take an introverted view of defence: "How is my family affected here in our own little plot?" Several of the articles in this edition of *Jane's Naval Review* have been chosen to explain the error of this attitude, and to show that while the world remains a very large place for merchant fleets and naval forces, we cannot afford to ignore events on the other side of the globe. The first, by the Commander-in-Chief US Pacific Command, describes the immense sweep of that command, from the East African coast to the West Coast of the USA. He emphasises the vast flow of trade in the Pacific area and its importance to the USA. "But what has that to do with us?" say some Europeans. The answer is simple: as has been proved twice already this century, the well-being of the USA is vital to that of the Western countries and of the non-Soviet states of the Orient and South Pacific. The conditions in these regions are examined in detail in this year's *Review*, as are recent events in the Persian Gulf and the Red Sea.

In these two stretches of reef-strewn water the consequences of state-sponsored terrorism have been clear for all to see. No longer is neutrality a shield for the world's trading ships; if the international law which protects them becomes inconvenient, those governments which nurture terrorism ignore it. Two and half thousand miles to the north, in the cold waters of the Baltic, a similar indifference to the normal standards of international behaviour is regularly shown by the Soviet forces which penetrate the territorial waters of neutral Sweden. The first of the two articles dealing with this problem shows the difficulties experienced by the Swedes. The second, a chilling and factual presentation, not only demonstrates what faces the people of the Baltic but is also a warning to all those who seek to protect their freedom. Any government which breaks faith with its people by neglecting its primary task, their defence, lays them open to incursion, disruption and, eventually, occupation.

Norway faces just such a threat, and Harold Ronneberg is well justified in the strong words he addresses to NATO: he saw it all before when Hitler's men arrived 44 years ago. While Ronneberg deals with one particular and vital segment of the NATO area, Sir James Eberle tackles the wider canvas of the Alliance command structure. Other commentators deal in detail with the three major navies of NATO, those of the USA, France and Great Britain, and Lord Lewin defends the recent reorganisation of Britain's Ministry of Defence.

Problems of commmand, control and communications of the kind alluded to by Lord Lewin and Admiral Eberle have bedevilled many a campaign over the last 3,000 or more years. The following lines, written about the 1809 campaign at Walcheren, could easily be applied to more recent conflicts:

> *Great Chatham with his sabre drawn*
> *Stood waiting for Sir Richard Strachan;*
> *Sir Richard, longing to be at 'em,*
> *Stood waiting for the Earl of Chatham.*

Many who have been engaged in war of one kind or another will recognise the situation. But today we are not at war; instead we hope to deter it by preparedness. Sound organisation to prevent waste of time and money is a necessary basis for this condition.

Little need be said of the last six articles. In an unsettled world it is good sense to know as much as possible about the country which stands to gain most by provoking instability and which has developed a fleet capable of exploiting such upheaval. What is offered here is a glimpse of the latest developments within a Soviet Navy that is large, effective and still developing rapidly.

John E. Moore
Elmhurst, Rickney,
Hailsham, Sussex

Counterbalancing the Soviet Navy East of Suez

Adm William J. Crowe Jr USN

The sphere of responsibility of United States Pacific Command (USPACOM), stretching from the US west coast to the east coast of Africa and including the Pacific and Indian oceans, is an area of growing strategic importance, not just to the US and its regional friends and allies but to all Free World nations. Asian and Pacific developments are having a profound effect on US security and the prospects for world peace and stability. Indeed, no effort to promote these conditions can be effective if it fails to account for the military, economic and political importance of the Asia/Pacific theatre.

Equally important is an understanding of the key role of sea power in achieving these goals. Most historians agree that a fundamental lesson of both world wars was that the United States, if seriously opposed at sea, cannot either project its own power to foreign shores or buttress its allies without first controlling the oceans. Nothing has happened since the Second World War to change this view.

Vietnam and Korea may have obscured this lesson for the United States, since we faced no opposition at sea. But 95 per cent of the material employed in both of those conflicts arrived by sea, and naval firepower was

employed to great effect. In Vietnam, and during the earlier Cuban missile crisis, naval interdiction proved highly effective. Sea control was also central to British success in the Falklands War, in which Argentina's lack of an effective ASW capability permitted a few Royal Navy attack submarines to keep the entire Argentinian Navy out of the battle.

Should the Free World be compelled to oppose the Soviets in a global confrontation, our ability to prevail at sea would be crucial. There can be no better example of this need for sea power than America's Pacific theatre of operations.

Economic and political realities

One good measure of the area's value is its growing place in the world's economic order. For example, the

---

Heading picture **The aircraft carriers USS** *Enterprise* **(CVN-65), USS** *Midway* **(CV-41) and USS** *Coral Sea* **(CV-43) and their respective battle groups, along with Canadian and Coast Guard forces, form up to kick off Fleetex 83-1 north of Hawaii on April 10, 1983. (***US Navy***)**

United States trades more with its Asian-Pacific neighbours than with any other region on earth. This commerce now accounts for over 30 per cent of all our foreign transactions, and has exceeded our dealings with the European Economic Community for over a decade. As a consequence, our nation's economic well-being is heavily dependent on its Asian connections and promises to become even more so with every passing year.

Trade between the US and Japan, totalling $60 billion a year, represents the largest bilateral seaborne economic exchange in world history, outstripping our commerce with the United Kingdom, Germany and France combined. This relationship is almost totally dependent on the security of the sea lanes between the two nations. Were this link to be broken, the economic consequences would be severe. Given the interrelated nature of the world's economies – and the fact that 16 of the world's top 30 bilateral trade relationships involve either the United States or Japan – the impact of such a disruption would soon be felt internationally.

Similarly, the Republic of Korea, the ASEAN states, Hong Kong and Taiwan are leading Free World suppliers and customers. This is the only region in the world to have enjoyed over 10 per cent annual growth for a prolonged period, and this shows no sign of abating. Asian-Pacific nations also provide much of the Free World's production of such strategic commodities as rubber, chromium, tin, titanium and platinum. In addition, more and more nations are turning to Southeast Asia as an alternative source of oil.

Meanwhile, most of the petroleum produced in the Middle East passes through the Indian Ocean en route to Asian and European consumers. In fact, over half the oil imported by Europe today travels along sea lanes which lie in USPACOM's area of responsibility. The commerce between Asia and the rest of the world has become vital to global economic stability. Ambassador Mike Mansfield, US envoy to Japan, has said that the next 100 years will be the "Century of the Pacific".

If our Pacific and Indian Ocean highways were severed or we relinquished control of them to a hostile power, the resulting shockwaves would be felt across the globe. In essence, the health and survival of the politically diverse nations that comprise the Free World have become dependent on seaborne trade. The industrialised nations must have the oil and strategic commodities that flow along the Pacific and Indian Ocean sea lanes. The economic survival of most developing nations likewise relies on this trade. Clearly, freedom to use the seas can spell the difference between economic stability and chaos.

We must also ensure that the nations supplying our critical resources do not unwillingly fall under the influence of those who would cause us harm. Were the Free World to be denied access to the Pacific theatre's strategic resources, the battle could well be lost without

A CH-46 Sea Knight helicopter comes in to land aboard the US Navy amphibious transport dock USS *Cleveland* (LPD-7) off the coast of Hawaii. (*US Marine Corps*)

a single shot being fired. The promotion of stability and support for economic and social development projects are effective guarantees against this, as is a strong US military presence.

While democracy has had an uneven record in Eastern Asia, the general tendency has been towards stability and responsibility. Throughout the 1960s and 1970s much of the region – particularly the non-communist community – has achieved political maturity and progress. Nations that a few decades ago had had little experience of self-government now change administrations with little trauma, permit open dissent and participate responsibly in Free World international councils.

The United States has on occasion endured agony in Eastern Asia, but these developments suggest that we have done some things right. The lion's share of the credit for their progress goes to the nations themselves, but the US can claim to have been a contributor. Our patient policies of broad economic and political support are now bearing fruit. Similarly, we have made many friends among the uncommitted nations of the area which share our ideals if not commitments.

US military strength has clearly been an important element in this effort. The American military umbrella, including strategic nuclear forces, has permitted these societies to concentrate on internal developments and realise their potential. Other key elements of our military presence in the Pacific theatre are the forward-deployed forces, particularly naval and Marine Corps units afloat along the sea lines of communication and near the strategic choke points. They act as a daily reminder of the American commitment to preserving and promoting stability in Asia.

The Soviet challenge

The Soviet Union, though well aware of the region's importance, has been largely unsuccessful in expanding its influence. Moscow's break with Beijing represents the Soviets' important setback, shattering the image of the Kremlin as the sole protector and interpreter of Marxism/Leninism. With the exception of Indochina, Soviet-sponsored communist insurgencies have generally stuttered if not disappeared altogether, leaving a residue of suspicion of Russian motives and methods. Quite simply, the growing stability and affluence of the free nations has made them less and less vulnerable to Soviet blandishments, ideology and intimidation.

Even the Soviets' successes are tarnished. They are buying Vietnamese friendship at the cost of $3–5 million a day. This money also underwrites Hanoi's repression of the Khmer people, which has harvested little goodwill for Moscow. Afghanistan can hardly be classified as a success in either political or military terms. North Korea, although friendly, is neither a grateful nor a reliable ally. These nations apart, the Soviet Union has gained little in Eastern Asia or on the Indian Ocean littoral, while incidents such as the ruthless destruction of the Korean airliner do further harm to their image.

The Russians have also been remarkably ineffective in penetrating Asia's markets. Only seven per cent of their exports go to the Pacific, and that vast area supplies only 12 per cent of their imports. Nor have their clients done any better: as the economies of the Republic of Korea, Japan, Taiwan and the ASEAN nations keep expanding, North Korea, Vietnam and Afghanistan are suffering from long-term stagnation or decline.

A landing craft from the US Navy's landing ship dock USS *Monticello* (LSD-35) hits Bellows Beach on Oahu in support of an amphibious assault. The morning assault against Bellows Air Force Station tested Navy/Marine Corps teamwork during the 1st Marine Brigade's Exercise Kernel Blitz. (*US Marine Corps*)

Frustrated by its poor economic and political performance, Moscow has turned more and more to the one tool that it can develop and exploit unilaterally: military strength. The Soviets apparently hope to gain through the threat or, as in the case of Afghanistan, the use of force the influence that has otherwise eluded them. As a result, despite our preoccupation with the threat in Europe and the Middle East, the huge increase in Soviet offensive capability in the Pacific and Indian oceans is emerging as the most far-reaching military development of recent years.

Over the past decade and a half the Russians have carried out an impressive force expansion and modernisation effort in the Soviet Far East. Ground force strength in the military districts adjoining the USSR's Asian frontiers has more than doubled. The modernisation programme has resulted in the Far East becoming a "state of the art" theatre. And they have established the command and control apparatus – in the form of a Far Eastern high command – needed to permit large-scale operations in Asia at the same time as a major conflict in Europe.

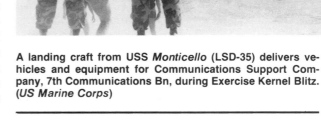

A landing craft from USS *Monticello* (LSD-35) delivers vehicles and equipment for Communications Support Company, 7th Communications Bn, during Exercise Kernel Blitz. (*US Marine Corps*)

The amphibious element of USMC Battalion Landing Team 3/3 advances toward the beach for an assault. The landing took place at the Barking Sands Missile Range on Kauai, Hawaii. (*US Marine Corps*)

In the 1970s the Soviet build-up was primarily a matter of increased numbers, and the threat from China figured largely though not exclusively in the equation. In recent years, however, there has been a new emphasis on power-projection forces capable of threatening all of Eastern Asia and non-Soviet forces in the theatre.

About a third of the launchers for the much publicised SS-20 nuclear missile have been deployed in the Far East; this provides for over 400 warheads. There has also been a steady increase in the number of fighters, attack aircraft and bombers. All told, there are about 2,500 combat aircraft in the area. Operating from the Soviet Union, longer-range types such as the Backfire bomber could attack bases and sea lanes as far away as Southern China, Midway, Guam and the Philippines and return without refuelling. The Aleutians and portions of mainland Alaska are also within Backfire range. Should these sophisticated aircraft deploy to Arctic forward bases, the Alaskan pipeline, the sea lanes over which oil travels from Alaska to American consumers, and portions of the Western US could also be threatened.

Most dramatic of all has been the build-up in naval power. The Pacific Fleet, already the largest in the Soviet Navy, has continued to expand and modernise to the point where it now represents over 30 per cent of the USSR's total naval assets. Included in its ranks are two out of three operational aircraft carriers, about 120 submarines (over half of them nuclear-powered), and a third of the Navy's attack aircraft, which are land-based. This expansion is all the more remarkable in view of the Soviets' long-standing preoccupation with the ground battle. It took 20 years, a growing global role, skilful political manoeuvring by Admiral Gorshkob, and repeated demonstrations of the value of Western sea power to change the Soviet hierarchy's attitude to maritime affairs. But once gained, the Kremlin's support has been unwavering. Historians may well conclude that the most remarkable military achievement of this era has been the transformation in two decades of the Russian coastal defence force into a sophisticated blue-water navy capable of global operations.

The Soviets have not hesitated to demonstrate their power-projection capability in the Pacific. In fact, nowhere is Soviet sea power displayed more regularly and impressively than it is within the USPACOM area of responsibility. Naval Backfires now routinely operate over the Sea of Japan and the Northern Pacific. They have been observed conducting simulated strikes against a US carrier battle group in the Northern Pacific. On any given day, 50–60 Soviet naval units are operating throughout the Pacific and Indian oceans. These forces include patrolling Yankee and Delta-class ballistic missile-equipped submarines. The Deltas, with their extended-range multiple-warhead missiles, represent a particular challenge, since they can strike virtually any target in the theatre or in the continental US from Soviet home waters or adjacent seas.

Russian intelligence-collectors also routinely patrol throughout the theatre: near US West Coast naval bases and operating areas, off Hawaii, Guam, Kwajalein and the Aleutians, off China's Hainan Island in the South China Sea, and in close proximity to the rest ot the theatre's strategic straits and choke points. Oceanographic research ships and submarines continue to "survey" the entire region, including the breadth of the South Pacific.

The Soviets have maintained a continuous naval presence at Vietnam's Cam Ranh Bay since the spring of 1979. It now amounts to 20 or more ships. Bear long-range reconnaissance aircraft have been based in Vietnam for several years. Badger bombers have recently been added in the first foreign deployment of long-range strike aircraft since 1972. These forces pose a direct threat to US naval and air facilities in the Philippines and along the sea lines of communication in that part of the world.

Meanwhile, the Soviet Navy has obtained what seem to be unrestricted basing rights in South Yemen and Ethiopia in support of an expanded naval presence in the Indian Ocean. Upwards of 25 Soviet ships will be found in close proximity to the Northern Arabian Sea and Indian Ocean trade lanes on any given day. The Red Sea naval repair facility on Ethiopia's Dahlak

Marines from Detachment Coy A, 3rd Amphibious Assault Bn, storm ashore in their Amtracs. (*US Marine Corps*)

Marines from the Third Marine Regiment, the major ground element of the First Marine Brigade, located at Marine Corps Air Station Kaneohe, Hawaii, take a long look at what will be their home for a while during a rotational deployment to the Western Pacific. (*US Marine Corps*)

Island helps to sustain this presence. Soviet attack submarines now also routinely patrol in both the Northern Arabian Sea and South China Sea. There is little Soviet commerce for these ships and submarines to protect, and in time of conflict they would probably attempt to play a "spoiler" or sea-denial role.

This presence, combined with the stationing of about 60,000 Soviet military and civilian advisers and technicians in many of the nations in or bordering on the USPACOM region, is clearly designed to intimidate states outside the Soviet bloc. In short, the Kremlin is making vigorous efforts to upset the balance in the USPACOM area, to extend the potential battle zone further from home, and to achieve by the threat of force the influence which has eluded them in the diplomatic and economic arenas.

Moscow can be expected to encourage and exploit dissidence, turbulence and overt conflict between states. Similarly, if they could attain unquestioned military pre-eminence the Soviets would be in a position to intimidate or divide their opponents. Let there be no mistake: the Soviets will not hesitate to use their

power brutally and directly when they believe the odds are in their favour – as witness Afghanistan. The US posture in the Western Pacific is therefore critical, since only America is strong enough to deter armed Soviet interference. Without US sea power, the security of the Free World's Asian lifelines could be in serious jeopardy.

The US response

In the wake of Vietnam there were grave doubts among many Asians (and others) as to American credibility and constancy. Since 1975, however, the US Government has made vigorous efforts to reaffirm its commitment to Eastern Asia. The decision to withdraw American troops from Korea was cancelled. Washington's links with Japan, the Republic of Korea, the Philippines, the ASEAN nations and the ANZUS alliance have been broadened and tightened. Our programme of ship visits has been expanded. Overtures to China are beginning to bear fruit. All told, these steps have resulted in our relationships with both allies and friends being perhaps closer today than they have been in many years.

Nor has America been standing still militarily. A variety of new weapons systems have been introduced. *Ohio* and *Los Angeles*-class submarines, *Spruance*-class destroyers and *Oliver Hazard Perry*-class frigates are

joining the fleet in increasing numbers, while Navy F-14s, USMC F/A-18s and USAF F-15s and F-16s add to our strength in the air. USAF E-3A airborne warning and control platforms have proven their ability to work closely with both USAF and naval air forces. The introduction of the nuclear-powered aircraft carrier *Carl Vinson* and the return to active duty of the battleship *New Jersey* (shortly to be followed by *Iowa* and *Missouri*) – with Harpoon and Tomahawk missiles to complement her 16in guns – increases the weight of fire and power-projection capabilities of the US Pacific

Tanks from the USMC's 2nd Platoon, Coy B, 1st Tank Bn, are safely placed on the beach by Navy landing craft during Exercise Bell Volcano in July 1984. The tanks formed the nucleus of an armoured assault force that came ashore on Kahoolawe before making its way to objectives inland. (*US Marine Corps*)

The battleship USS *New Jersey* (BB-62) steams off the West Coast of the United States. *New Jersey* was recommissioned on December 28, 1982. (*US Navy*)

Fleet. Finally, theatre war reserves – ammunition, sustainables and petroleum stocks – are now climbing.

As Secretary of the Navy John Lehman has pointed out, "The course to re-establish maritime superiority has been set, and we are well along the way. We have achieved an effective balance between building for the future and making the fleet we have today a ready-fighting force. The results achieved have added enormously to our deterrent capability. The fleet and the fleet marine force are more ready to go in harm's way than at any time in post-war history."

The nearly 360,000 men and women assigned to USPACOM are as good as any I've seen in my 40 years of service. Our soldiers, sailors, airmen and marines are professional in every sense of the word. They're well educated, bright, dedicated and hardworking, and possess a genuine sense of purpose. In fact, if we enjoy a marked advantage over our potential opponents in any area, it is in the quality of our personnel.

Over half of the Pacific Command is deployed outside the continental United States. Two of our three Marine Corps amphibious forces are in the Pacific, divided between the US and Okinawa. The Army's 2nd Division is stationed in Korea and the 25th Infantry Division is quartered at Schofield Barracks, Hawaii. The US Air Force has four active-duty tactical fighter wings dispersed over the Western Pacific. About half of

An F-14A Tomcat from the US Navy's Fighter Squadron 124. (*US Navy*)

our naval forces are assigned to the theatre, with the Third Fleet based in Hawaii and the Seventh Fleet forward-deployed in the Far East.

Strategic Air Command maintains a wing of B-52 bombers and KC-135 tankers on Guam. In addition to their primary strategic role, these bombers have worked closely with USPACOM conventional forces, particularly in the maritime surveillance role. B-52s regularly conduct multiple-refuelling "round-robin" missions into the Indian Ocean in conjunction with our naval battle groups. The sight of a B-52 overhead, 5,000 miles from the nearest available base, serves as an effective indication to Soviet naval units (and other potential adversaries) of US commitment and capability. B-52s also operate over the Eastern Pacific and in Northern Asia, and train for a variety of missions, including minelaying and other maritime support operations.

In response to recent events in the Middle East, the Seventh Fleet maintains a carrier battle group in the Indian Ocean to demonstrate our commitment to keeping our lifelines and strategic choke points open to commerce. In addition, we periodically sail an amphibious ready group to that area with 1,800 fully equipped Marines embarked. The prepositioning of ships loaded with ammunition, equipment, fuel and drinking water at Diego Garcia allows the rapid introduction of additional forces in time of emergency.

Underpinning these efforts is an extensive base structure in Japan, Korea, Guam, the Philippines and Hawaii. This network permits us to sustain our forces in the Western Pacific and Indian Ocean, to maintain a presence astride the sea lanes, and to be in a position to respond promptly to potential crises.

Our forward-deployed strategy has served both the United States and its allies well. But we must not underestimate the task ahead. The increasing threat and the years of neglect that plagued our military establishment after the Vietnam War took a painful toll of our capabilities. Recent improvements notwithstanding, it will be several years before the current modernisation programmes are completed and our major deficiencies corrected. The Defence Department has mapped out a long-term effort designed to restore the margin of superiority which we require to counter the expanding Soviet threat, and it is imperative that we stay the course. Nowhere will the return on this investment be greater than in the Pacific.

Regional co-operation

The day when the US could or should go it alone has passed. The most effective means of countering the growing challenge to peace and stability worldwide is a concerted effort on the part of all peoples who cherish their independence. I sense a gradual realisation of this fact in Asia, and a growing willingness to seek co-operative solutions to common problems.

Within the Pacific Basin the US has formal security agreements with six countries: Japan, the Republic of Korea, Thailand, the Philippines and Australia and New Zealand (ANZUS). However, our interests are not limited to formal allies. For instance, we encourage the Five-Power Defence Arrangement (FPDA), which links Australia, New Zealand, Great Britain, Singapore and Malaysia. Similarly, we support the Association of South-East Asian Nations (ASEAN), which comprises Thailand, Malaysia, Singapore, Indonesia, the Philippines and Brunei. These collective efforts contribute heavily to the peace, prosperity and stability of the region.

Among my command's contributions to these alliances is a vigorous programme of combined exercises, designed primarily to increase the ability of the participating countries to meet their own defence

The newest type to join the Pacific Air Forces is the A-10 Thunderbolt close support aircraft. PACAF's A-10s belong to the 25th Tactical Fighter Squadron, a tenant unit at the Republic of Korea's Suwon Air Base. (*US Air Force*)

The 961st Airborne Warning and Control Squadron, equipped with E-3A Sentries, was established in May 1980 at Kadena Air Base, Japan. Its primary mission is to provide additional command and control resources in the Pacific and to permit a quick response to any contingency or crisis in the theatre. (*US Air Force*)

A US Air Force F-4 seen from the boom operator's station in the Strategic Air Command KC-135 tanker that has just refuelled the fighter. The F-4 crew, taking part in the Pacific Air Forces' most frequent exercise, Cope Thunder, is now ready to acquire simulated combat experience at the Crow Valley range in the Republic of the Philippines. (*US Air Force*)

A US Air Force F-15 from Kadena Air Base, Japan, prepares to take on fuel from a Strategic Air Command KC-135 during a Cope Thunder exercise. (*US Air Force*)

requirements. But they also establish close ties between my headquarters and foreign military organisations and lay the groundwork for increased co-operation with US forces in the event of general hostilities.

Defence of sea lanes is stressed during these exercises. Of particular note was Fleetex 83, a combined US/Canadian effort which involved the first triple carrier battle group operation in the Northern Pacific since the Second World War. Held just south of the Aleutian Island chain, the manoeuvres involved 40 US Navy ships and hundreds of Navy and Air Force aircraft, along with US Coast Guard and Canadian naval units. The co-operation and interoperability demonstrated by USAF and USN forces was especially encouraging. About 23,000 American and Canadian servicemen participated in this demonstration of resolve to protect the approaches to North-east Asia and the North American mainland.

We give our fullest encouragement and support to Japan's willingness to improve its ability to defend its North Asian sea lanes. Evidence of this is Japanese participation in the RIMPAC exercise series, which combines Australian, New Zealand and Canadian naval forces.

The relationship of China with US and Free World interests must also be understood. The four-million-man Chinese Army is a key factor in deterring further Vietnamese aggression. Hanoi's worries about a renewed border war with China have compelled it to base about half of its military strength along the country's northern border. These forces could otherwise be diverted to Kampuchea or elsewhere in South-east Asia. Similarly, I am persuaded that China does not

Principal role of this US Air Force F-16 Fighting Falcon, from the 8th Tactical Fighter Wing at Kunsan, Korea, is ground attack. The F-16 also has a significant air-to-air capability. (*US Air Force*)

desire another Korean war and acts as a restraining influence on Pyongyang.

More importantly, the Chinese provide a significant counterbalance to the Soviet military build-up in Asia. About 90 per cent of the Soviet Union's Far Eastern ground forces are arrayed against China. The uncertainty over China's role in any global conflict ensures that these troops will not be used elsewhere in Asia or redeployed to Europe. While China is not a US ally, our nations have many parallel interests, including our mutual concern over the expansionism of the Soviet Union.

Addressing the Washington Press Club recently, US Defence Secretary Caspar Weinberger said: "A strong, secure and independent China is a positive force for peace and stability." He further noted that "China has moderated its foreign policies and demonstrated a real desire to improve state-to-state relations with its Asian neighbours." We should reinforce these encouraging trends and capitalise on our common interests.

Such efforts must also include military assistance to our friends and allies. Their strength complements and multiplies our own and contributes significantly to stability. Defence co-operation throughout the Pacific Command area has never been better: we should now do everything possible to build a lasting security assistance policy on this foundation.

The South Korean Army's II Corps and Hawaii-based 25th Infantry Division soldiers paddle across the Han River in Korea during Exercise Team Spirit 84 acclimatisation training. (*US Army National Guard*)

Infantrymen from Combat Support Company, 1st Bn, 25th Infantry Division, based at Schofield Barracks, Hawaii, live-fire a TOW missile during Team Spirit 84. (*US Army*)

Chill winds in the North-west Pacific

Kensuke Ebata

Moscow turned its attention to the Pacific in the middle of the 1970s and the Soviet Pacific Fleet has been steadily increased since then. The most spectacular advance was the assignment of two VTOL aircraft carriers, *Minsk* and *Novorossiysk*, to the fleet. *Minsk*, which has been assigned to the Pacific since 1979, did not return to Soviet Europe as expected when *Novorossiysk* was first deployed to the Pacific in late 1983. The Soviets have been continuously expanding the facilities in Cam Ranh Bay, Vietnam, and their presence in that area now exceeds ten vessels at any given time. Cam Ranh Bay has clearly been established as the forward base of the Soviet Pacific Fleet for operations in the Indian Ocean. The fleet now has over 90 major surface combatants and about 170 submarines, of which half are nuclear-powered, according to Admiral William J. Crowe, C-in-C US Pacific Fleet. He revealed these figures at the joint US-Japan defence talks held in Honolulu, Hawaii, last June, adding that about 80 Tu-22M Backfire bombers of the Soviet Air Force and Naval Aviation are now deployed in the Far East.

The Soviet Union has also been increasing its influence in North Korea, and Najin, the city nearest the border with the USSR, has become virtually another Soviet forward base. Although the USA has been doing her best to maintain the naval balance in the West Pacific with the assignment of the new nuclear-powered aircraft carrier *Carl Vinson* to the Pacific Fleet and the strengthening of the Naval Surface Group

Heading picture The design of the Chinese Luda class of destroyers (foreground) was probably based on that of the Soviet Kotlin class, which was under construction in the USSR when Sino-Soviet relations were still cordial. The Chinese ships are larger, however, with many differences in the superstructure. No 105 was lead ship, and the subsequent 13 units (with more building) show several variations. By the standards of the leading navies their electronic fit is largely out of date and their fire-control systems rudimentary. Of 3,900 tons full load, and armed with four 130mm guns and 16 of smaller calibres, these are the largest warships in the PRC Navy. They were also the first to be armed with SSMs, carrying six Hai Ying 2 derivatives of the Soviet SS-N-2. The second ship in this line-up is the first of the Jiangdong class of frigates, completed in 1977. She and her sisters were designed to be the first SAM-armed Chinese ships but this programme has been much delayed.

Zhongdong, first of the Jiangdong class, is shown here with two *Anshan*-class destroyers in the background. The Jiangdong class has the same 2,000-ton hull as the Jianghu class, which now numbers 15 ships. The latter class is equipped with four SSMs in place of the SAMs intended for the Jiangdongs. In each case two diesels give a speed of about 26kt. The *Anshan* class, now three ships, is particularly notable for its antiquity, all the ships being ex-Soviet *Gordy*-class vessels completed over 40 years ago. All were converted between 1971 and 1974 to carry four SSMs.

Western Pacific by replacing *Knox*-class frigates with *Spruance*-class destroyers, Japan, South Korea and China are uneasy about the Soviet Navy's rapid expansion in the region.

These countries cannot strengthen their naval power at will, however. China and South Korea are short of money while Japan, in economic power second only to the USA among the nations of the Free World, is hampered by strong domestic objections to increased defence spending.

China

The People's Republic of China has now supplemented her ICBM deterrent force with nuclear-powered ballistic missile submarines. The PLA recently established a strategic missile force and the Navy has at least one Xia-class SSBN, and possibly two. The 8,000-ton Xia carries 12 to 16 1,800nm-range CSS-NX-3 SLBMs. There is no indication that the CSS-NX-3 carries MRVs or MIRVs, so the Xia class seems to be similar in capability to the US *George Washington* class, commissioned in the early 1960s. It is believed that the class will eventually run to about six boats.

China has also been putting great efforts into the building of the Han-class nuclear attack submarines (SSN), though technical and financial problems have resulted in severe delays. The first boat appears to have been completed in 1974 and the second in 1977. There have been references to a third boat but no evidence that it has been completed. There is however no positive reason to believe that the programme has been halted.

The production of conventionally powered attack submarines (SS) is also very slow. Two Ming-class SS are reported to have been completed in the middle of the 1970s, but there is no evidence of any follow-on boats and it seems that this 1,900-ton teardrop-type design is a failure. Thus the Chinese Romeo-class SS remain the main force of the world's third strongest submarine fleet, and building continues. As many as 92 Romeos have been completed, but they will have to be replaced from the late 1980s if China is to maintain an effective submarine force. Conversion of some of the Romeos to the cruise missile role, reported in 1983, is possible if China is willing to trade diving performance for a new capability. It is most unlikely that China has developed a compact Tomahawk-type cruise missile, and the modified Romeos would probably end up resembling the Soviet Twin-Cylinder Whiskey class.

China is said to have started building aircraft carriers. Such ships would be extremely valuable to the Chinese Navy, which would use them for SSBN and fleet air cover, anti-submarine warfare, and power projection in support of diplomatic efforts. But the country's current economic and technological shortcomings would seem to rule out something as complex and expensive as a carrier even if it were of the comparatively small V/STOL type. It is however possible that studies are being carried out with a view to a go-ahead when conditions permit.

In 1983 *Zhongdong* appeared with this radar set, which was believed to be unique in the Chinese Navy until a second was seen on a Luda-class destroyer. It appears to be a form of 3D air-search system.

high public confidence in her SAM systems – the ground-based types at least – as recently reported by the New China News Agency. A new, possibly indigenous three-dimensional phased-array air-search radar has been observed on the Jiangdong and Luda classes. No details have emerged, but its existence shows that the Chinese are trying to develop even the most advanced systems themselves, apparently utilising technology steadily transferred from the West.

Powerful surface combatants equipped with effective anti-ship, aircraft and submarine weapon systems are urgently needed to counter the massive build-up of the Soviet Pacific Fleet. The Luda, Jianghu and Jiangdong classes are at present inadequate to the task, and will remain so as long as money and technology are in short supply.

Coastal defence suffers from the same problem, and no significant modernisation has been carried out. The expected Hola-class missile FAC did not enter serious production, and the ageing Soviet-designed Osa (Chinese Huangfen) and Komar (Chinese Hegu) classes are still the mainstays of the Chinese coastal defence force.

Not all is gloom in Chinese naval circles, however. A number of large, modern support ships appeared in the

Her financial problems also forced China to cancel the contract with British Aerospace for the modernisation of the Luda-class destroyers, and now the Ludas and the Jianghu-class frigates are being fitted with modern systems of indigenous origin.

Only two Jiangdong-class SAM destroyers have been observed, and the effectiveness of the missile system remains an unknown quantity. However, China shows

This is one of the Chinese Hainan class of fast attack craft (patrol). Construction of this 392-ton, 30kt class has been under way for 20 years. The hull form is similar to but larger than that of the Soviet SO 1 design, later craft showing variations from the original plan. The two twin 57mm mountings, two 25mm mountings, four anti-submarine rocket launchers and associated sonar, mine rails and depth charges make this an effective general-purpose patrol craft. Examples have been exported to Bangladesh, Egypt, North Korea and Pakistan.

Fiji area for the ICBM test launches in 1980. Building of the Fuqing-class replenishment oilers continues, three ships having been completed. The Dajiang-class submarine support ships are remarkable by any standard. Though the Chinese still lack the combat stores ships, ammunition ships and oilers needed for long-range operations, the existence of a large number of research and survey ships clearly shows that they intend to develop a deep-sea navy.

China's leaders must be concerned about the slow pace of naval modernisation, but matters cannot improve until the country's financial and technological resources are expanded. SSBNs apparently consume a large part of the naval budget, but the project will not be abandoned, however expensive it becomes. China will continue her efforts to obtain Western technology at minimum cost. The visit of US Navy Secretary John Lehman to China in August 1984 may prove to be the trigger for a speeding-up of the modernisation of the Chinese Navy in the near future.

Taiwan

Taiwan is well positioned to control the sea lanes between the East and South China seas and to deny the Soviet Pacific Fleet access to the Indian Ocean. This island nation has however been suffering severe economic problems since the late 1970s. No major warship project has been started during this time, nor will be in the future. Two Improved *Zwaardvis* conventionally powered attack submarines have been ordered from Wilton Fijenoord in the Netherlands, and after much diplomatic debate they are to be delivered in 1985 and 1986. Taiwan may now be seeking another supplier of submarines, her option on a second pair of boats having been cancelled by the Dutch Government under pressure from China. A solution to this problem might lie in co-operation with Israel: both nations are looking for similar answers, and they have assisted one another many times in the past. Whatever the outcome, any country trying to sell submarines to Taiwan will face opposition from China. This will cause much heart-searching in the West, for a powerful Taiwanese submarine force would surely be a valuable contribution to Free World security.

Taiwan's main surface force still consists of ex-US *Gearing*, *Allen M. Sumner* and *Fletcher*-class destroyers. Though most of them are 30 years old, they are receiving a valuable increase in capability in the form of Hsiung Feng (Taiwanese version of the Israeli Gabriel) SSMs and Sea Chaparral SAMs. Nonetheless, Taiwan is struggling to maintain the effectiveness of her surface fleet, and new surface combatant projects must be launched soon. The alternative is a further deterioration in Taiwan's international position, particularly in relation to China, and a still greater degree of isolation.

Han Yang (foreground) is one of 13 ex-US *Gearing*-class destroyers operated by Taiwan. In addition to four 5in guns and an assortment of short-range weapons, all this class is being fitted with the Hsiung Feng II SSM, an adaptation of the Israeli Gabriel. All ships carry a hangar and helicopter and six anti-submarine torpedo tubes, while nearly all have an Asroc mounting.

It is reported that a new-design corvette was completed in 1983, though no details are known. Her appearance suggests a displacement of around 1,000 tons, but no major weapon system is fitted. Even if a number of these ships are built, Taiwan will still be a long way from having anything more than a coastal navy.

The US-designed PSMM-5 missile FAC project was terminated with only two craft completed to make way for the less expensive and smaller Hai Ou class. The Hai Ous, equipped with two Hsiung Feng SSMs, might be effective for coastal defence but would be of little value for deep-water operations.

Taiwan still maintains a sizeable though obsolete amphibious force. Though these ships have been maintained for the unrealistic purpose of "recapturing the Chinese continent," it would be politically inexpedient to delete a large number of them. But unless Taiwan releases naval funds by deleting old and increasingly ineffective amphibious ships, she will not be able to modernise her fleet.

▲Needing a cheap means of getting lots of SSMs to sea, Taiwan designed the 47-ton Hai Ou class of missile craft. This photograph shows six of the 34 so far built at a rate of about eight a year. Each craft carries two missiles and a 20mm gun. Two diesels give 36kt, and complement is only 10.

▼The Taiwanese amphibious force is impressively numerous, even though the majority of the 28 landing ships and 150 craft of US origin are now 40 years old. The 280 Taiwan-built craft are appreciably younger. The photograph shows *Chung Chuan* (ex-US LST-1030), now in her 41st year. (*L. J. Lamb*)

Japan

The Japanese are at last appreciating the importance of sea-lane defence to the security of their country, with its huge industrial capacity and almost total lack of raw materials. Six hundred million tons of imports a year are needed to keep Japan alive. The Japanese Maritime Self-Defence Force (JMSDF) and Air Self-Defence Force (JASDF) have been given budget priority in recent years. The 1981 Mid-Term Defence Programme Estimate ends this fiscal year, to be succeeded by the 1984 estimate. The 1981 plan projected 15 destroyers and frigates, five submarines and 12 minesweepers. Though the building programme has been delayed by defence spending restraints the JMSDF modernisation programme has proceeded steadily. The JMSDF plans to have four escort flotillas, each consisting of one helicopter destroyer (of the 4,700-ton *Haruna* class or 5,200-ton *Shirane* class), two missile destroyers

One of the failures of the Japanese Naval Command in 1941–45 was its inability to appreciate the proper use of submarines. Since then the Japan Maritime Self-Defence Force has built a series of submarine classes of increasing capability. *Takashio* (shown here) is the sixth of the *Uzushio* class, the first of which was commissioned in 1971 and the seventh and last in 1978. Of 2,430 tons dived displacement, these boats can cope with the frequently appalling weather conditions found in Japanese home waters and have a dived speed of 20kt. The succeeding *Yuushio* class is slightly larger and is commissioning at a rate of one a year. (*Ships of the World*)

(3,950-ton *Tachikaze* class or a new 4,500-ton class) and five multi-purpose destroyers (2,950-ton *Hatsuyuki* class or 3,400-ton Modified *Hatsuyuki* class). Each helicopter destroyer carries three HSS-2B Sea King ASW helicopters and each multi-purpose destroyer one HSS-2B. Thus one escort flotilla will deploy a total of eight large ASW helicopters; the 4,500-ton missile destroyers are also to have a helicopter deck, providing additional platforms.

Four helicopter destroyers were completed by 1981 and the first pair, *Haruna* and *Hiei*, are to receive modern electronics and point-defence systems. The modernisation of *Haruna* is to be completed in 1988 and her service life is to be extended from 24 to 32 years. Similar modernisations are being applied to the four *Takatsuki*-class multi-purpose destroyers. The first ship, *Kikuzuki*, is to complete her modernisation in 1986, having received two quadruple Harpoon SSM launchers, one Phalanx 20mm CIWS and a Sea Sparrow octuple launcher. The Dash unmanned ASW helicopter facilities and aft 5in gun are to be removed. Modern electronics, including towed-array sonar, are also to be fitted. *Kikuzuki* and *Takatsuki* are being

Shirane is one of the two largest ships in the JMSDF. At 5,200 tons full load, they each carry three anti-submarine helicopters, two single 5in guns, a Sea Sparrow SAM launcher, a 20mm CIWS, an Asroc launcher and six anti-submarine torpedo tubes. Two steam turbines give a speed of 32kt. (*Ships of the World*)

Sawakaze is the third ship of the 4,700-ton *Tachikaze* class of destroyers. Commissioned in March 1983, she was the first of the class to be fitted with the Harpoon SSM; the other two ships are to be retrofitted. The powerful armament fit of these 32kt ships is completed by a Mk 13 launcher for Standard SAMs, an Asroc launcher, two 5in guns and six anti-submarine torpedo tubes. (*Ships of the World*)

The *Yamagumo* and *Minegumo* classes of destroyer (nine in all) commissioned between 1966 and 1978. *Yamagumo* (shown here) was the first of this design of diesel-propelled ships to have a primarily anti-submarine armament. (*Hachito Nakai*)

modernised under the 1981 estimate, with *Mochizuki* and *Nagatsuki* following under the 1984 estimate.

Though the JMSDF's surface combatants are currently short of air-defence capability, improvements are in hand, with all of the major surface combatants to be fitted with SAMs. Following the three *Tachikaze*-class Standard-armed missile destroyers, the first of the new COGAG-powered 4,500-ton missile destroyers was laid down in May 1983. To be completed in March 1986, it will be equipped with the Standard missile system, two 5in guns, one Asroc launcher, two quadruple Harpoon SSM launchers, two 20mm Phalanx CIWS and two triple ASW torpedo tubes. Funds for the second ship were authorised in FY 1983 and two more are to be requested in FY 1987. The JMSDF is said to be considering the fitting of the US Navy's Aegis air-defence system to these two ships. The displacement with such a fit would be 6,500 tons.

A total of 13 ships of the *Hatsuyuki*/Modified *Hatsuyuki* class have been completed or are being fitted out, and another ten of the latter are planned under the 1984 estimate. The Modified *Hatsuyuki*s have a larger standard displacement (3,400 tons) than the original class (2,950) tons as a result of the use of steel in place of

The Japanese designed the *Chikugo*-class frigates in the mid-1960s. There was then a pause until May 1979, when the single *Ishikari* of 1,290 tons was laid down. In February 1981 she was followed by *Yubari* (shown here), first of a new class of 1,490-ton small frigates. With eight Harpoon SSMs, a 76mm gun, a Bofors anti-submarine launcher, six torpedo tubes and a CODOG powerplant giving 25kt, these are useful ships in Japan's enclosed waters. (*Hachito Nakai*)

aluminium in the superstructure and an enlargement of the hull. It is significant that in the HSS-2B (Mitsubishi-built Sea King) these comparatively small destroyers carry a large ASW helicopter equipped with a dipping sonar. The construction of missile destroyers and multi-purpose destroyers has taken precedence over the building of frigates. Only two frigates, of the *Yubari* class, were authorised in FY 1979 and 1980 even though the JMSDF urgently needs these modern gas turbine-powered (CODOG) frigates as replacements for the ageing *Isuzu*-class frigates and small submarine-chasers. The design of the *Yubari* class and their prototype ship, *Ishikari*, puts emphasis on surface attack rather than ASW capability, though they carry

one quadruple Bofors ASW rocket launcher and two triple ASW torpedo tubes each. Two quadruple Harpoon launchers provide a very effective coastal defence capability. A new frigate with a displacement of 1,900 tons will be requested in FY 1985. Among the weapons being considered for it is the General Dynamics RAM anti-SSM system.

The JMSDF wants to build FACs to replace the present force of five elderly torpedo boats. But the programme has been delayed every year, partly because of the lack of a clear idea of how they should be used and partly because funds were not available. Harpoon-armed hydrofoil FACs were considered but rejected because of their high cost of building and operation and their low endurance. A small, 120 tons displacement, FAC was also evaluated but again rejected, this time on account of its poor seakeeping in

Hiyodori is included as an illustration of the speed with which change has encompassed the JMSDF. This 440-ton ship and her remaining sisters are about 20 years old and outmoded, with a speed of 20kt and a minimal armament. (*Ships of the World*)

the heavy seas around Japan. The JMSDF is considering a request for a 250-ton FAC in FY 1987. It would be powered by high-speed diesels instead of gas turbines.

The JMSDF has a powerful and modern conventional submarine force currently totalling 14 boats and, the service hopes, rising to 15 in the near future. Funding is a problem, however. Two *Asashio*-class non-teardrop submarines need to be replaced. Authorisation of two boats a year over the next few years is essential if a 15-submarine force is to be achieved, but current budget allocations make this unlikely. Nevertheless, the submarine force has been steadily improving. The fifth boat of the *Yuushio* class – *Nadashio*, commissioned in March 1984 – can launch Sub-Harpoon. Follow-on boats are to have the same capability, and there will be retrofits for the earlier boats of the *Yuushio* and *Uzushio* classes. Equipped with automatic three-dimensional control, engine remote control and ZYQ-1 digital information-processing, and incorporating high-tensile steel structure and teardrop hull design, the JMSDF's new submarines are highly effective. Construction of a new, 2,400-ton, class is planned in the 1984 estimate.

The JMSDF has one of the most effective mine countermeasure forces in the world. The minesweeping force was the core of the original JMSDF and has been operating ever since the end of the Second World War. Indeed, 40-year-old US land mines are still to be found in Japanese waters. Eleven *Hatsushima*-class 440-ton minesweepers have been built under the 1981 and preceding estimates, while the 1984 plan allows for a new 1,000-ton design. This class will carry a full range of modern minesweeping and hunting gear. Means of countering deep-sea mines are receiving special emphasis, and development of the S-7 and S-8 hunting/sweeping systems is to start next year. Six 1,000-ton minesweepers are planned.

The JMSDF has long been reluctant to introduce GRP hulls for its minesweepers because of the shock-transmitting characteristics of this material when mines are detonated. But now GRP minesweepers have been introduced into the next defence build-up budget. The introduction of minelaying aircraft, possibly C-130s, has received a lot of consideration but for financial reasons has not materialised.

The JMSDF has an inadequate force of support ships and auxiliaries in general and fleet replenishment ships in particular. Only two fleet support ships, the oiler *Hamana* and the combat support ship *Sagami*, are in commission, and one 8,300-ton fleet replenishment ship, the replacement for *Hamana*, is to be laid down soon. The need for such ships is not seen as pressing, since in a crisis the JMSDF could make use of the huge

The tanker *Hamana* (shown here) was for a long time after her commissioning in 1962 the only indication that the JMSDF might recognise a need for support beyond its home ports. Though she has now been joined by the 5,000-ton fleet support ship *Sagami*, Japan still has far too few auxiliaries for a fleet which is now expected to operate 1,000 miles from its bases. (*Ships of the World*)

Uraga is one of a growing class of 3,700-ton patrol ships in service with the Japanese Maritime Safety Agency (coast-guard). All the larger ships of this force of over 400 ships and craft are armed and can carry a helicopter.

Takuyo is the largest and most modern of the 25 ships and craft of the hydrographic service of the JMSA. Completed in 1983 and with a full-load displacement of 2,979 tons, she has a huge range of 16,000 miles at 17kt.

Japanese merchant fleet, even though no contingency plan exists at present. The same is true of the transport force. The JMSDF has only six medium-sized LSTs and two small (590 tons) LSUs. The nation's defence strategy does not call for a powerful amphibious force, and in an emergency a number of Ro-Ro ships and LASHs from the merchant fleet would provide a very effective transport capability.

The purchase of 75 P-3C ASW aircraft has been authorised and the service hopes to increase the

number to 100. No other country in the world except the USA has as many shore-based ASW patrol aircraft. The JMSDF is to introduce the SH-60B shipborne ASW helicopter as the successor to the HSS-2B, and a total of 12 MH-53E minesweeping helicopters are due to replace the existing V-107s.

The JMSDF continues to have budget-related problems – among them low ammunition stocks – but the government's new attitude to maritime defence means that the force modernisation has been proceeding steadily. Development of new systems, including torpedoes, mines and radars, is planned. Further integration with the other two services and the Japanese Maritime Safety Agency will give Japan a large and effective maritime defence capability in the 1990s. But will the service be able to cope with the tremendous threat presented by the deployment of Soviet nuclear aircraft carriers to the Pacific Fleet in the late 1990s?

South Korea

South Korea has similar problems to Taiwan, both economic and strategic, though the South Korean economy is not as strained as that of Taiwan. Facing the massive submarine threat of North Korea, the republic needs its own submarines, if only to act as targets during ASW training. The reported building of 175-ton small submarines in South Korea reflects this requirement. The South Koreans also continue to negotiate with West Germany on the purchase of two Type 209 submarines, with an option on building more under licence. Submarine operations around the Korean Peninsula would probably be limited by the shallow waters of the area, but the possession of submarines would make South Korea better able to bar the Tsushima Strait to the Soviet Pacific Fleet, as well as countering the North Korean submarine force.

Confronted with the North Koreans' large force of FACs the South Korean Navy has been putting

emphasis on the fitting of SSMs (Harpoon and Standard) on her surface combatants. Two ex-US *Gearing*-class destroyers are now equipped with Harpoon launchers, and eight PSMM-5 FACs carry either Harpoon or Standard.

South Korea has no strategic need for a deep-sea navy and so has concentrated her resources on new frigates and corvettes of comparatively short range. The first indigenous frigate, *Ulsan*, was completed in 1981 and carries four Exocet SSMs, two 76mm Oto-Melara guns, eight 30mm machine guns and two triple ASW torpedo tubes. It is reported that three more ships of this class are under construction. The corvette programme calls for a total of 11 1,400-ton (full load) ships, of which four have been completed. The corvettes are not as technically interesting as the frigates, but they nevertheless reveal the growing capability of South Korea's warship yards. The country has now become a major exporter of naval ships, principally to South American and Asian states.

The lack of an air-defence capability in most surface combatants might not prove serious as long as they operate under Air Force cover. The major weakness is an inadequate mine-warfare force, amounting to only eight ex-US minesweepers. Some of these vessels are comparatively modern but the rest are over 25 years old. If North Korea were to use her large number of small craft and submarines to lay mines, South Korea would have little way of clearing her port approaches. Nor could she expect aid from the US Navy's mine countermeasures force, which is also under strength. The South Korean Navy has a large amphibious force,

As Western shipyards jockeyed for orders east of Suez, South Korea made her bid for the business with designs such as the 2,000-ton frigate *Ulsan* (shown here). The fact that she has an aluminium alloy superstructure suggests that she may suffer from stability problems.

Close on the heels of *Ulsan* came the HDP 1000 class from the same yard, Hyundai at Mipo Bay. Of 1,400 tons displacement, these ships have an unimpressive armament fit.

though all the ships are now around 40 years old. While there is no current operational reason for such force, South Korea's experience in building LSTs for export would permit a rapid modernisation programme if required.

South Korea expects the 1988 Seoul Olympic Games to accelerate the expansion of her economy, as with Japan after the 1964 Tokyo games. If this is the case, more defence funding will be available and the expanding merchant fleet needed to serve a growing economy will in its turn require a navy capable of deep-water operations.

North Korea

Following last year's bomb outrage in Rangoon, North Korea has found herself more isolated than ever. Aid from China has diminished and so has Chinese influence. On the other hand, relations between Pyongyang and Moscow have been developed steadily. The port of Najin has seen more and more Russian traffic and is now virtually a Soviet naval base. A number of MiG-23 Floggers have been delivered, and it is possible that the North Korean Navy has also received Soviet equipment.

Reports of North Korea building small submarines have been current since the first half of the 1970s, and the Navy has long been using midget submarines for incursions into the South; some of these craft have been captured by South Korea. The large submarine force, comprising 15 Romeo class and four Whiskey class, is not particularly efficient but it does continue to pose a threat to other Far Eastern countries.

North Korea has been trying to build surface combatants to an indigenous design. The Sariwan-class patrol craft and Chodo-class FACs, built in the 1960s, have little value other than for coastal patrol. They were followed by the larger and more effective 1,500-ton Najin-class frigates, only two of which have been completed. It is reported that at least one of them has been modified to carry SS-N-2A SSMs. There is no indication that North Korea is building further ships of this class or starting work on any new class.

The large missile FACs transferred from the USSR need to be replaced, possibly by the Soju and Sohung classes. The former is a modified version of the Osa class and carries four SS-N-2s, while the latter is a variant of the Komar class. The first of both classes was completed in 1981 but the building rate is very slow. North Korea has a massive force of small coastal craft which might be effective for supporting an invasion of the South but would have little effect on the naval balance in the West Pacific. The strategy behind the disproportionately large submarine fleet is also very questionable.

The economic situation of North Korea is very unsatisfactory, and there can be little hope of improvement as long as the country's leaders persist in their present attitudes. These will attract further aid and influence from Moscow, resulting in still more instability in the peninsula, with all that that implies for peace in the Far East.

South-east Asian allies pushing hard for readiness

A. W. Grazebrook

Over the Allied South-east Asian (ASEAN) nations hangs the threat of open war as a result of Vietnam's persistence with military action in Cambodia which spills over into Thailand. On top of this, in four of the five nations of ASEAN (Indonesia, Malaysia, the Philippines, Singapore and Thailand) there is insurgent action which is being countered by military force.

Vietnam maintains an army as large and powerful as that which existed at the end of her fight against the United States, and covets the resource-rich islands of the South China Sea. Steadily and methodically, the Vietnamese Navy is being transformed from the collection of obsolete Second World War craft inherited in 1975 into a powerful force with the ability to deploy

missile-armed fast attack craft, supported by heavily armed, fast light frigates, across the comparatively short distances of the ASEAN region.

Refugees from Vietnam are the prey of another maritime threat – pirates. After a century or more of inactivity pirates are becoming a significant threat not

Heading picture Canberra is the second in a class of four frigates built in the USA between 1977 and 1984 to the American FFG-7 design. This purchase meant that at least four RAN ships would be able to operate ASW helicopters at sea, a capability that would have been lost following the cancellation of the carrier programme. Two more modified FFG-7s are to be built at the naval yard at Williamstown, Victoria. (RAN)

only to refugees in small, unseaworthy craft but also to merchant shipping. Thai pirates are active in the Gulf of Thailand, while other pirates prey upon merchant ships in the Malacca Straits and South China Sea littorals.

Thailand has to deploy naval forces in the Gulf of Thailand and, together with her ally Malaysia, against Communist insurgents in the Kra Isthmus. The unhappy state of the nations surrounding the Bay of Bengal has reminded Thailand that she too borders on this body of water. Consequently, the Thais have built a small operating base for her naval forces on her west coast.

Indonesia still has East Timor festering in her midst. Her population redeployment programme has caused unrest in West Irian and border friction with Papua New Guinea. A nation of a thousand islands cannot help but depend upon maritime communications, which are particularly vulnerable to internal or external threat.

Internal unrest is growing in the Philippines, which is also a nation of many islands and vulnerable maritime internal communications. Fighting insurgents requires patrol vessels and the means of deploying and supporting ground and air forces.

In the face of these current and potential threats the nations of ASEAN (with the exception of the Philippines) are well advanced in the development of their maritime forces. Malaysia's balanced naval development programme is proceeding well. The first pair of a planned four frigates have been launched and are now in service. A small fleet air arm has been formed to provide these ships with helicopters. Construction of the first four of a planned eight new minesweeper/hunters is well advanced in Italy. Two fine 1,800-ton support ships have been commissioned for training and light craft support duties. A new small underway-replenishment tanker has been launched in the Republic of Korea, from which Malaysia has also ordered a pair of tank landing ships to replace two of Second World War vintage. Four more missile-armed fast attack craft are being built. Discussions with potential suppliers of medium-range diesel-electric submarines have begun, with a view to acquiring a means of striking back at Vietnam.

Sea Wolf, commissioned by Singapore in 1972, was the first of six Lürssen TNC45 missile craft. Displacing 230 tons, they carry five Gabriel missiles and single 57mm and 40mm guns. With a maximum speed of 38kt, these craft could operate among the islands at the narrowest part of the entrance to the Malacca Strait, carrying out interdiction patrols.

The division of Malaysia into Peninsular Malaysia, with coastlines totalling about 1,300 miles and fronting both the Malacca Strait and the South China Sea, and Eastern Malaysia, covering 1,600 miles of the northern and north-east coasts of Borneo, could not be more inconvenient for naval operations. Support ships are therefore vital, and the first, *Sri Indera Sakti* (shown here), was commissioned in 1980, with two more following in 1983 and 1984. They can support light and MCM forces, carry 80 or more troops, perform command and control functions, transport vehicles, and refuel and operate helicopters. (*C. Gee*)

With her new main naval base at Lumut now virtually complete, Malaysia is forging ahead with her naval development programme. The only apparent gap is the lack of a replacement for her numerous and necessary patrol boat force. It is possible that the Malaysian customs service will assume more of the patrol function.

Although Singapore is not a nation to neglect her defences, it is now four years since she ordered new naval vessels. Consideration is however being given to the acquisition of new gun-armed fast attack craft for use in the anti-piracy role and for joint operations with Singapore's SSM-armed fast attack craft. Though Singapore's tank landing ships have been extensively refitted, they were built during the second World War and cannot remain operational much longer. Her two 30-year-old minesweepers are reported to have been stripped of their MCM gear and put to use for general training. With her waters so eminently mineable, Singapore would be well advised to follow the example of her neighbours and build new minehunter/sweepers.

Further south, Indonesia continues to replace the ships and submarines acquired from the Soviet Union in the late 1950s and early 1960s. Extensive building programmes overseas are being supplemented by the domestic construction of smaller craft. There are plans to extend this activity, as the reorganisation of the

Thailand has three comparatively modern frigates. *Tapi*, shown here, displaces 1,135 tons, has a maximum speed of 20kt, and carries two 3in and two 40mm guns, Hedgehogs and anti-submarine torpedo tubes. Six other frigate-sized ships are listed, but they are all long overdue for replacement.

In 1972 *Perdana*, the first of four 265-ton missile craft built in France, was accepted by Malaysia. Four more missile craft were delivered from Sweden in 1979. The French boats carry two Exocet SSMs each and the Swedish boats four. Also on Malaysian strength are a total of 22 large patrol craft, six gun-armed fast attack craft and four frigates. *(G. K. Jacobs)*

Malaysian coastal waters, with an average depth of no more than 50m, are particularly conducive to mine warfare. Until 1982 the Malaysian Navy's MCM capacity resided in a decreasing number of ex-British Ton-class minesweepers. These were replaced by four Italian *Lerici*-class minehunters, the first of which, *Mahamiru*, is shown here. Peacetime tasks include offshore patrol, for which they will carry two 40mm guns instead of the single 20mm in the Italian Navy version. (*Intermarine*)

Daring is one of six Vosper Thornycroft gun-armed fast attack craft to enter service with Singapore in 1971–72. Supported by 12 46-ton coastal patrol craft, they represent a capability which, even in peacetime, is probably well stretched by the increasing incidence of piracy in the area.

Surabaya dockyard testifies. Her many islands create a need for amphibious operations, and Indonesia is exploiting to the full the five new LSTs built in South Korea. Each of these ships operates three Super Puma troop-carrying helicopters.

Indonesia clearly found her Yugoslav-built training frigate an operational asset. CODOG-powered and equipped with SSMs, guns and a helicopter, this ship has clear advantages, particularly when her accommodation for an extra 114 training personnel is used for troops or marine commandos. Indonesia's second such ship is expected to complete shortly. This pair will be joined by three Tribal-class frigates bought from Great Britain. Indonesia already has Wasp helicopters for these ships. A further four SSM-armed 290-ton fast

attack craft have been ordered from South Korea, and two gun-armed 396-ton fast attack craft from West Germany. Indonesia has taken an option on the building of another six of these craft at Surabaya. Indonesia's patrol capacity is being augmented by the acquisition of light aircraft and helicopters, including Nomads from Australia.

Mystery surrounds Indonesia's submarine-building programme. Two boats have entered service, but the status of the remaining four is unknown. Industrial sources describe these boats as "still under discussion". Plans for two command frigates have been deferred. However, the three Dutch-built CODOG-driven corvettes are heavily armed and well able to support Indonesia's force of SSM-armed fast attack craft. The reported acquisition of at least four Italian-built *Lerici*-class MCM vessels demonstrates that Indonesia is alive to the threat of the mine, which in this case is particularly potent.

Unavoidably involved as she is with Vietnam's action in Cambodia, Thailand is struggling with some success to find the funds needed to build a navy capable of dealing with that of Vietnam, countering the piracy that is rampant in her waters, and supporting counter-insurgency operations in the Kra Isthmus. Two new, powerfully armed 825-ton corvettes have been ordered from the United States. These ships will be armed with Harpoon SSMs, Albatros SAMs, anti-submarine torpedo tubes and a 76mm gun, and will provide formidable support for Thailand's squadrons of missile and gun-armed fast attack craft. The British-built frigate *Makut Rajakumarn*, now ten years old, is to be modernised and her anti-aircraft armament enhanced. A number of much needed large patrol craft and small landing craft are under construction in Thailand. Four

Excellence is one of six ex-US 511-1152 LSTs acquired by Singapore since 1971. All but one have been modernised since 1977. *Excellence* is the only example with a helicopter deck. (*G. K. Jacobs*)

GRP-hulled mine countermeasures craft are reported to be on order from Italy.

First funds for two or possibly three submarines are expected to be provided in 1985. Discussions with potential builders, including HDW in Germany, are under way.

Beset with political and economic problems, the Republic of the Philippines is having great difficulty in funding new equipment for her elderly but much needed navy. With virtually all her larger vessels of Second World War vintage, the term "block senility" is a better description of the problem than "block obsolescence." So far only three SSM-armed fast attack craft and a number of large patrol craft have been ordered, from local Korean and West German sources. The growing internal conflict places heavy demands on the elderly tank landing ships in service. So far one new LCT has been built in the Philippines and more are believed to be under construction. The Navy is known to be seeking new frigates but funds are not available. However, like the other ASEAN navies, that of the Philippines has clearly identified its strategy and knows what is needed to implement it.

To the south of ASEAN, Australia is in serious difficulty with her maritime defences as a result of strategic indecision and misconceptions. At the root of these difficulties lie two factors:

In 1976–80 Thailand acquired six missile craft to act as the front line of the light forces. *Chon Buri*, a 30kt gun-armed fast attack craft, is one of the most modern.

The remainder of the Thai light forces comprise 94 patrol craft varying from 450-ton large patrol craft to 8-ton river craft. Shown here are two of the 35-ton, 25kt coastal patrol craft forming part of a programme begun by Ital-Thai Marine in 1980.

• the decision to acquire a new carrier, subsequently rescinded by a new government
• the commitment of a very high proportion of defence funds to the F/A-18 Hornet fighter programme.

Australia's navy had been authorised to acquire a new aircraft carrier from which to operate her eight Sea King helicopters; these aircraft are a vital link in the country's anti-submarine defences, providing long-range guidance for the Ikara anti-submarine missiles upon which most of Australia's escorts depend. The decision not to acquire a new carrier keeps the Sea Kings ashore and restricts Australia's most potent surface anti-submarine weapon to very short ranges. This problem is exacerbated by the delay in ordering helicopters for the four US-built *Oliver Hazard Perry*-class frigates which have now joined the RAN, an omission which deprives these ships of anti-submarine capability and over-the-horizon guidance for their Harpoon SSMs.

Seriously compounding the situation is a lack of both fighter cover and mine countermeasures capability.

The decision not to order a new carrier and the subsequent sale of the Fleet Air Arm's A-4 Skyhawk fighter-bombers to the Royal New Zealand Air Force leaves the Australian Navy dependent upon the Air Force's Mirage squadrons for fighter cover. These units lack the range, reaction time and specialist training needed for this task. Even when the Hornets arrive later in the 1980s, range will be limiting in the attack role and reaction times will be far too long to permit the provision of effective fighter cover where it may be needed: over the Arafura Sea, for instance or the trade routes of the Indian Ocean.

The third serious gap, the lack of a mine countermeasures capability, is not the result of strategic

Thailand's shallow waters make mining a major threat. *Donchedi* is one of four ex-US *Bluebird*-class coastal minesweepers, now 20 years old. Along with five minesweeping boats and an MCM support ship, they represent the total Thai MCM capability. Four new vessels are reported to be on order.

definitely, by a lack of design personnel. These two problems mean that Australia will have no credible mine countermeasures capability at least until 1990. Ironically, there is no dispute about the strategic need for MCM, and the funds are being made available.

Apart from its effect on naval air power, the F/A-18 cost problem has had an impact on other programmes. The building of a second *Durance*-class underway replenishment ship in Australia has been postponed for at least five years, as have two further five-boat batches of *Fremantle*-class patrol craft. However, *Success*, the first under-way replenishment ship, is now due to commission early in 1986, and *Darwin*, the fourth *Perry*-class frigate, has commissioned in the United States. *Darwin* is an example of the larger variation of the *Perry* design and is thus capable of operating SH-60B-sized helicopters. Two further ships are to be built in Australia. The first keel will be laid in July 1985 for completion in 1991. These two ships will be of the same size as *Darwin* but will have the Australian-designed Mulloka sonar. Until they receive effective helicopters the first four frigates will have Aerospatiale Squirrel helicopters for utility and flying training purposes.

Consideration is now being given to the next generation of escort ship. The naval staff requirement is understood to call for a ship of some 3–4,000 tons incorporating the extra anti-aircraft capability necessitated by the lack of fighter cover.

confusion. Rather, development and administrative difficulties have afflicted an innovative effort to build GRP catamaran-hulled inshore minehunters. As a result, the last wooden-hulled coastal minehunter will pay off for disposal well before even the two prototype inshore minehunters are launched. The acquisition of coastal minesweepers has also been delayed, in-

Oxley was the first of six *Oberon*-class submarines built in Greenock for the RAN. Originally similar to boats of the same class in the Royal Navy, the Australian submarines have been greatly improved by the fitting of a Singer Librascope fire-control system, Sperry passive ranging sonar, Krupp attack sonar, US Mk 48 torpedoes and, in 1985, encapsulated Harpoon missiles. (*RAN*)

An earlier purchase from the USA was the three-ship *Perth* class of 4,618-ton destroyers, built to a modified *Charles F. Adams* design. *Perth*, the first, is now nearing her 20th year since first commissioning, and *Hobart* (shown here) is only six months younger. Since 1974 a series of major refits and modernisations have resulted in the fitting of updated radar, electronics, gun mounts and missile control systems. (*RAN*)

Torrens, built at Cockatoo Island, Sydney, and commissioned in January 1971, is the last of six River-class frigates built to two different designs based on the British Type 12 and *Leander* classes. The first four of the Rivers have been subjected to half-life modernisations lasting 4½–5 years. *Torrens* and *Swan* are to have a major refit instead of this modernisation. (*RAN*)

Tobruk, the RAN's single amphibious heavy-lift ship, can carry 350–500 troops, a squadron of tanks, artillery and vehicles. But what will stand in for her if a crisis occurs while she is laid up for refit or repair? (*RAN*)

With a 16,000-mile coastline to cover, the RAN's hydrographers have an immense task. Their ships are all modern and purpose-built but few in number. *Cook* (shown here) joined *Moresby* and *Flinders* in 1974 after a building and trials period prolonged by numerous defects. The elderly *Kimbla* has now been deleted, while the two survey ships foreshadowed in the 1976 White Paper have not materialised. Four 120-ton survey launches, planned for completion in 1987–88, will provide welcome extra capacity for inshore work. (*RAN*)

Modernisation of the River-class (modified Type 12) frigates is proceeding, although lack of money has reduced the extent of the work on *Swan* and *Torrens*. Nevertheless, these two ships will receive Mulloka and their Mk 10 mortars will be replaced by Mk 32 anti-submarine torpedo tubes.

The sixth *Oberon*-class submarine weapons update programme will be completed in 1985, and planning and design work on a new generation of diesel-electric submarine is going ahead, with two designs to be selected for detailed development. The first boat is to enter service in 1991. The naval staff requirement calls for a submarine comparable in size and capability with the Dutch *Walrus* design, to be armed with Mk 48

New Zealand's hydrographers have a less extensive task than their Australian counterparts but it is nevertheless a taxing one. In 1974 the Cook Islands service ship *Moana Roa* was taken over and converted into the 3,900-ton survey ship *Monowai*. She operates with two 92-ton inshore survey craft. (*J. Mortimer*)

Four Lake-class 134-ton large patrol craft (*Rotoiti* shown here) were commissioned into the RNZN in 1975. Although built to a standard Brooke Marine design they are too small for effective patrol in the very heavy seas often encountered off the New Zealand coast. (*L. & L. van Ginderen*)

torpedoes and encapsulated Harpoon missiles, or derivatives of these two. The new boats will probably be built in Australia.

New Zealand and Australia have signed an agreement under which the former will participate in the study stages of Australia's new submarine project. This follows New Zealand's Defence Strategy Review, which was approved by the previous government and is understood to have support from the new one. The review looked ahead to the block-obsolescence problem that will arise when all four of New Zealand's anti-submarine frigates reach retirement age in the 1990s. It is proposed to replace them with four diesel-electric submarines which would be identical in design, armament and sensors to Australia's new boats. They would be complemented by two surface vessels, described as support ships, which would provide some degree of forward logistic support and carry out surveillance work, surface training and other tasks.

Meanwhile, the two oldest Type 12 frigates have been withdrawn from service, while *Canterbury* and *Waikato* remain in the fleet. The commissioning of HMS *Dido* as HMNZS *Southland* has added Ikara to the RNZN's armament and brought a degree of commonality to the RAN and RNZN – an objective which has received little more than lip service in the past. HMNZS *Wellington* (the former HMS *Bacchante*) is rapidly approaching the completion of her modernisation at Auckland.

The review acknowledges the need for MCM but plans to leave this task to the Reserve, which although very capable will find the role very difficult without equipment (about which the review is disturbingly vague).

New Zealand's decision on whether to switch to submarines, involving as it does a major strategic change and reduction in anti-submarine capability, will not be taken for another two years. Money problems rather than strategic considerations are the driving force. In the meantime, the resulting period of uncertainty and divisive debate will be very unsettling for the New Zealand Defence Force. It will also add to the worries of both Australian and New Zealand commanders, already troubled by Australia's lack of fighter cover, helicopters and mine countermeasures capability.

Venezuela's first-class little navy

Dr Robert L. Scheina

One cannot help but be impressed with the Venezuelan Navy. It has some of the most modern hardware in the world and yet is only 10,000-strong (including marines), making it a small-sized navy by world standards. Equipment comprises six *Lupo*-class frigates; two Type 209 submarines and an old Guppy; six large patrol boats, three of which are armed with Otomat surface-to-surface missiles; and three modern LSTs (due to be delivered in 1984) plus other craft to give an amphibious dimension to a 4,000-man marine corps.

Counting units is not however a very reliable gauge of potential performance. Many small navies have some modern hardware, but do they know how to use it and is the equipment operational or available only for naval reviews and parades? The evidence that the Ven-

ezuelan Navy is a first-class fighting machine is over-whelming. If one reviews the Caracas newspapers and other sources, it becomes apparent that Venezuelan naval units spend much time on manoeuvres and training. Since 1959 the United States Navy has trekked around Latin America and held "Unitas" combined operations with most Latin American navies. Initially Venezuela's participation was very modest, amounting only to a manpower contribution in the early days. But

Heading picture Three *Lupos* wait at Roosevelt Roads Naval Base, Puerto Rico, before taking part in the 1984 Unitas exercises. Venezuela has six of these ships. (*Dr Robert L. Scheina*)

At the heart of the Venezuelan surface fleet are six *Lupo*-class frigates, represented here by *General Urdaneta*. These well armed ships carry both surface-to-surface and surface-to-air missiles. The Venezuelans have successfully fired live missiles of each type. (*Dr Robert L. Scheina*)

An Agusta-Bell AB-212 lands aboard the *Lupo*-class frigate *Almirante Garcia* during exercises in July 1984. This helicopter can provide mid-course correction for the Otomat surface-to-surface missiles carried by the ship, extending their range well beyond the horizon. (*Dr Robert L. Scheina*)

since then this south American republic has played a larger and larger part, culminating in 1984 in the appearance of three *Lupo*-class frigates – *General Urdaneta*, *General Salom* and *Almirante Garcia* – and the Type 209 submarine *Sabalo*. Perhaps even more important, for the past few years the Venezuelan Navy has regularly exercised with the other armed forces in the course of the "Falcon" operations. Air Force aircraft have had an opportunity to practise against the fleet and vice versa. These manoeuvres pre-date the South Atlantic conflict of 1982, in which the Argentinian armed forces learned this lesson the hard way.

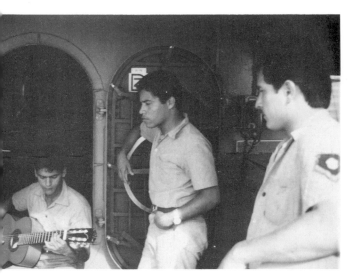

Conscripts relax aboard the *Almirante Garcia*. These men had to volunteer for an additional six months' duty – 24 rather than 18 – in order to enter the Navy instead of one of the other services. (*Dr Robert L. Scheina*)

The Venezuelan Navy's successful firing of live missiles in recent years is impressive for a force of its size. Early in 1982 the *Lupo*-class *Mariscal Sucre* successfully fired an Otomat Mk 2 surface-to-surface missile over a range of 131.5km to strike the target ship *Falcon* (ex-USS *Robert K. Huntington*). Mid-course target information was supplied by an AB-212 helicopter flying from the *Sucre*. In 1983 the *Almirante Garcia* earned itself a "Long Rifle" certificate when it shot down a drone with an Aspide missile during that year's Unitas operations. There is strong evidence that other live missile and torpedo firings have taken place recently.

What is the key to the Venezuelan Navy's high state of operational readiness? Undoubtedly the service's extensive educational system has made a major contribution and it warrants close examination as a model for other small navies. For our purposes naval personnel may be divided into four groups: conscripts, enlisted personnel, warrant officers and officers. A Venezuelan citizen has an obligation to serve for 18 months in the armed forces. If he wants to enter the navy he must have a primary education certificate – seven years of schooling – and he must agree to serve 24 months. The conscript receives four and a half months of training at the *Escuela de Grumetes*, located at La Guaira near Caracas, and then he joins an operational unit. Those conscripts who choose to continue in the service after their conscription return to La Guaira and enter the *Escuela Tecnica*. Course length depends on the speciality but typically ranges between six months and a year. If the individual fails to complete the course

A Venezuelan technician works on a torpedo at Puerto Cabello Naval Base. (*Dr Robert L. Scheina*)

he is obliged to leave the service. If he is successful he advances into the enlisted ratings and signs a two-year contract. He may ultimately become a chief petty officer, retiring after 26 years of service.

Also located at La Guaira is the warrant's officers' school. Students with three years of high school and aged between 16 and 19 can compete to embark on this three-year course. They may choose among various specialities such as machinery, logistics, armaments and administration. The individual holds a commission from the government similar to that of an officer and is obliged to serve at least five years. He may advance through six grades of warrant during his career and can retire after 33 years of service.

Potential Naval Academy cadets must have completed high school, which takes five years in Venezuela. The first two years of the four-year Academy course are devoted to general studies. For the next two years each student must specialise in electronics, mechanics or logistics. After graduation from the Academy an officer receives additional education, frequently abroad, as he progresses through the ranks. For example, Vice-Admiral J. P. Fernandez Marques, the Chief of Naval Operations, attended the gunnery school in Britain in 1959–60, various command courses in France in 1969, and the National Defence College in Venezuela in 1977–78. The current Venezuelan Naval Attaché to the United States, Vice-Admiral Freddy Mota Carpio, has attended three advanced military schools in the USA, including an ASW warfare establishment.

When an officer leaves the Academy he chooses a speciality: the fleet, aviation, submarines or the Marine Corps. Some receive additional training: for example, those who choose aviation must first pass an exam before going on to specialised schooling, generally outside the country. The new aviator then returns to Venezuela, where he receives still more training before he is assimilated into the fleet.

Great emphasis is placed on the learning of English. Today 60 per cent of all officers understand English and 40 per cent can speak the language. Many manuals and instruction books are provided in English only in order to encourage the learning of the language.

An AB-212 about to take off from a *Lupo*. The seaman in the foreground mans a fire monitor. The safety precautions taken during flight operations are fully comparable with those of larger navies. (*Dr Robert L. Scheina*)

One of two utility landing craft recently constructed in the United States for the Venezuelan Navy. Venezuela has the fourth largest marine corps in Latin America; only those of Argentina, Brazil and Chile are bigger. (*Dr Robert L. Scheina*)

English is also used for communication on all multi-national naval exercises.

The system described above has succeeded in providing the Venezuelan Navy with a cadre of well trained enlisted and commissioned personnel. The navy in which they serve is highly efficient and rational in its structure. There are six administrative commands: Operations, Chief of Staff, Education, Logistics, Personnel, and Inspector General. Operations is divided into four major units: the Fleet, Marine Corps, Coastguard and Naval Aviation.

The Fleet has five squadrons: frigates, submarines, amphibians, support and patrol. The Marine Corps is made up of approximately four thousand men, comprising five battalions strategically located throughout the country. Its amphibious capabilities are currently being significantly increased by the acquisition of three new LSTs from Korean yards. The Coastguard is a relatively new command, having been created in the past few years. No two coastguards are alike; that of Venezuela is responsible for drug patrols, aids to navigation, search and rescue, and inshore patrol against infiltration. This last task accounts for the fact that the two *Almirante Clemente*-class frigates and six *Constitucion*-class patrol boats, three armed with Otomat missiles, are assigned to the force. In fact the Venezuelan Coastguard is a part of the Navy rather than a separate service, as is frequently the case in other countries, though it may evolve into one in the future. Its ships and craft bear the words "Guardia Costa" in

white on typical navy-grey hulls. At present its officers and men are naval personnel on regular rotational duty. The Naval Aviation Squadron was created in 1974 in succession to an aviation logistics group. The force currently flies six Agusta-Bell AB-212 helicopters, eight S-2E Trackers and 11 logistics aircraft. There are about 50 pilots.

The Anglo-American community has been quick to criticise Latin American nations for their lack of democracy and, in particular, the military for their role in politics. Most commentators can rattle off those countries which in their opinion are the most flagrant offenders. But can they also cite the success stories? Venezuela must be among the foremost. In 1959 the Venezuelan military, with the Navy taking a lead, removed one of the most corrupt dictators on the continent, Marcos Perez Jimenez. Since then Venezuela has had a democratic government.

Where does the Venezuelan Navy go from here? The country's "new frontier" lies to the south and is basically riverine in nature. The Navy will thus become increasingly involved in protecting national interests in the area. The acquisition of new equipment must

Lookouts aboard the *Almirante Garcia* watch a mock air attack on their task group by Venezuelan Air Force Mirages. The Venezuelan Navy regularly exercises with its sister services. (*Dr Robert L. Scheina*)

depend on the state of the economy. Venezuela, like most of Latin America, has a huge balance of payments problem, and in 1984 the currency was devalued. Nonetheless, national defence needs will not be ignored. Though it is likely that no new major fleet units will be acquired in the next five to ten years, probable developments include the establishment of new naval aviation bases, particularly in the southern part of the country; an increase in the numbers of naval aircraft, particularly patrol and logistics types; and the acquisition of small patrol vessels.

The Venezuelan Navy has made significant advances in professional quality during the past two decades. In spite of the current need for financial restraint the Navy will continue to grow stronger. Indeed, it has already become the strongest Caribbean navy apart from that of Cuba.

The bridge aboard a *Lupo*. (*Dr Robert L. Scheina*)

The Gulf: hazardous but still navigable

Capt John Moore RN

In spite of the attacks on neutral merchant shipping in the Gulf (see *Merchantmen in the Gulf front line*) and the resulting hefty increase in insurance rates, maritime business has continued more or less as usual. Contributing to this display of phlegm by the shipowners is the fact that there are a large number of ships laid up which could be used as replacements for those damaged or sunk. The attacks normally take place in the approaches to Bandar Khomeini and Kharg Island, both nodal areas for oil traffic. The Saudi action in shooting down Iranian jets which became overadventurous indicated a determination to restrict the attacks to the north-east coastal area. Once again, airborne early warning proved to be decisive.

The Iranian Government has threatened to block the Strait of Hormuz should she be prevented from exporting oil from Kharg Island (known as Jaz-ye Khark to the Iranians). Hormuz is the eastern entrance to the Gulf from the Gulf of Oman and the Arabian Sea between the Iranian port of Bandar Abbas to the north and the Musandam Peninsula in Oman. The deepwater channel between Jaz-ye Larak in Iran and the rocks off Didamar to the south is about 20 miles wide, with a deepest sounding of 89m and an average depth of about 60m. Blocking such a waterway presents a number of problems. The first method to be considered would probably be the use of mines. There is a widely held belief that the laying of mines is a simple operation, requiring only a small dhow and a few lusty seamen to toss the weapons over the side. Nothing could be further from the truth. Mines come in various shapes and sizes and vary a great deal in weight. Their methods of actuation dictate the depth of water in which they can be laid to operate effectively. Accurate navigation is essential if a minefield is not only to have a reasonable chance of success but also to be sufficiently well charted as not to present a danger to friendly shipping.

The two types most difficult to clear, the pressure and acoustic varieties, are of no use in water over 40–50m. This leaves the magnetic and horned-antenna contact mines, the former being either of the bottom or moored variety and the latter moored only. Some

Heading picture   Omani fast attack craft *Al Bat'nah*. (*J. L. M. van der Burg*)

magnetic mines can be effective if laid on the sea bed in about 150m, others require lesser depths. The deeper mines require larger charges and their total weight varies between about 1,200lb and a ton. The moored mines, be they magnetic or contact, require an anchor and weigh about a ton when fully assembled. None of these mines is of a size or weight to be manhandled; all need tracks, rails or a suitably converted aircraft. An effective field across a 20-mile-wide stretch would require something like 2,000 to 3,000 mines, the laying of which would take a long time particulary when under observation from the southern shore. There are however other types of mine which might be used. All are mobile in the water: the unanchored oscillating mine, the drifting mine attached to a float, and the creeping mine with a chain on the bottom to restrict its speed of movement. However, all of these would need frequent replacement as the local tidal streams moved them in or out of the Gulf.

Even if there were five lines of well laid moored mines the task of sweeping a passage in each direction would not be an insurmountable problem. The routes in the Traffic Separation Scheme (TSS) north of Didamar could be made safe within a matter of weeks, though this would depend on the ability of the Western navies involved to make the necessary ships available from their already slim mine warfare resources.

Sweeping operations could be put at risk by artillery mounted on the Iranian island of Jaz-ye Larak, some 10 miles from the northern limit of the TSS. Even a 100mm gun has a range of some 14 miles, while a 152mm at maximum range can reach the 20 miles across the Strait. However, any such attempt to disrupt mine clearance or bombard merchant ships would risk heavy air strikes from Western carriers in the Gulf of Oman, calling for both missile and gun AA defences. Thus any attempt to block Hormuz would require a significant diversion of effort and a great deal of planning and intensive training, and could well result in an unacceptable counter-strike.

Such a strike would be most effective if aimed at Bandar Abbas, the only well equipped Iranian port beyond Iraqi air cover except Chah Bahar, some 300 steaming miles to the east, close to the border with Pakistan and with a main exit road which runs but a few miles from the border with Afghanistan. Bandar Abbas is an important centre containing a commercial port, a naval base and an air base. Normally there are about 50 ships waiting to discharge at the commercial port, which is the main terminal for non-oil-related traffic in Iran. It is however also very vulnerable to attack from the sea. The Sultan of Oman's Navy could, if so minded, carry out an attack with 20 Exocet missiles

The current Omani royal yacht, equipped with helicopter pad and satellite navigation.

from its FACs, while a concerted Western air attack, centred on US carriers, would flatten the port facilities. Even the threat of such assaults would result in a rapid inflation of insurance rates and the paralysis of the Iranian import trade. Despite their reputation for religious fanaticism, the Iranian leaders are sufficiently pragmatic to have appreciated these facts.

The navy of Oman is in a commanding position on the southern side of the Strait of Hormuz. Omani ships and radar stations carry out continuous surveillance of the Strait from bases at Goat Island and Ras Mussandam. Apart from the navy's interest in protecting the territorial waters of the Sultan, it also maintains a watch on the TSS, assures free navigation in the Strait and keeps a weather eye on the interpretation of the term "innocent passage". The recent arrival of Oman's three 400-ton Province-class missile FACs has provided additional means of meeting national requirements and enforcing international law.

The Omani Navy is a highly trained and effective force with excellent morale and an increasing capability, qualities which can no longer be attributed to its Iranian counterpart. Since the departure of the Shah, senior naval officers have come and gone with a depressing regularity and inevitability. Afflicted with low-grade conscripts, overconfident officers, and an abrupt end to training and spares from the USA and UK, the Iranian Navy sank to a very low point a couple of years ago. During the war with Iraq a number of ships and craft have been lost, and it has since proved impossible to replace them. Some reports suggest that a certain improvement in the fleet's effectiveness has taken place recently, but then it could scarcely have become any worse. There is little regular Iranian naval activity in the Gulf. When the ships do appear they behave correctly and there is little sign of flamboyance or adventurism.

There is no indication of the Gulf War coming to an early end. On the other hand, the attacks on tankers seem unlikely to disrupt the oil trade, and as long as the Iranians have as much to lose as anybody from the closure of Hormuz, the Strait is likely to remain an unencumbered waterway.

The original Omani royal yacht, *Al Mabruka*, was completed in 1971. She was taken in hand in 1982 for conversion into an offshore patrol vessel with a secondary training function. (*W. Sartori*)

Merchantmen in the Gulf front line

Nigel Ling

The Iran/Iraq conflict has given rise to the unusual situation of neutral merchant ships manned by non-combatants being deliberately attacked by both belligerent nations. These attacks have been indiscriminate, often directed at vessels not trading with either combatant nation. A wide variety of air-launched munitions have been used, from cannon shells and unguided bombs to AM 39 Exocet air-to-surface missiles. The accompanying table gives details of the casualties recorded between March 30, 1984, and July 10, 1984. Reports inevitably conflict or are exaggerated, but the evidence available makes it possible to interpret some of the events and demonstrate the effects of modern weapon systems on ship structures.

The Iraqis were the first to begin attacking neutral shipping in open waters. They appear to have made extensive use of French-supplied Exocets, launched from Dassault Super Etendard naval strike aircraft and, possibly, Aérospatiale Super Frelon helicopters. The Iranians appear to have employed more novel

The effect of an Exocet on the starboard side of the engine room of the *Safina al Arab*. There were no casualties, and all but 10,000 tons of the 350,000-ton cargo was saved. But a depressed tanker market meant that the vessel was declared a constructive total loss, such was the estimated cost of structural repairs and renewal of the electronic equipment in this modern, highly automated ship. Note the clean shape of the hole created by the explosion of the missile's warhead, the plates apparently having torn along the welded seams. (*Smit International*)

▲ With the *Al Ahood* fire at its height, hoses are rigged as
salvage crews battle to prevent the flames from spreading to
the oil cargo. Portholes in the blazing superstructure can be
seen glowing through the black smoke. (*Selco*)

▶ Progress is being made as the spread of fire aboard *Al Ahood*
is checked and water is sprayed to cool the superstructure.
(*Smit International*)

Struck on May 8, 1984, by a missile which passed through the settling tanks and into the engine room, the Saudi tanker *Al Ahood* pours black smoke as she is towed to shallow water. The ship's oil tanks were cracked and the fire was oil-fed, which increased its intensity. A pool of burning oil can be seen on the surface of the water. (*Smit International*)

The crew of the salvage tug *Drado* spray foam onto the burning oil surrounding *Al Ahood* before going alongside to tackle the intense fire burning in the after part of the tanker. (*Smit International*)

The deck fires are out and the tug *Drado* smothers the starboard side of the superstructure with foam from her main monitor at a rate of 400m³/hr. (*Smit International*)

methods of air-to-surface attack. In addition to cannon fire, bombs and unguided rockets, Sidewinder infra-red-homing air-to-air missiles are said to have been used.

Following its employment by Argentina in the Falklands War the air-launched Exocet has once again proved the reliability and effectiveness of its guidance system. However, a loaded supertanker presents a very large radar image and no countermeasures have been employed, and so a large proportion of the weapons launched were going to find their targets. Moreover, the fuzing deficiencies that became apparent when the missiles hitting *Sheffield* and *Glamorgan* failed to explode have continued to be evident in the Persian Gulf.

The United States Navy recovered virtually intact the Exocet which caused only minor damage and no fire aboard the Greek tanker *Filikon L*. Other Exocets have caused fires and extensive damage. The most notable Iraqi success was the Yugoslav-manned bulk carrier *Fidelity*, loaded with steel, which sank with the loss of three lives.

The Iranians are widely reported to have fired heat-seeking missiles from F-4 Phantoms. These are almost certainly 75kg Sidewinder air-to-air missiles, set up to home onto the hot exhaust gases and engine rooms of the targets. There have been accounts of aircraft circling the target to put the sun behind them and come within the 1,100m sea-level range of the Sidewinder.

While crude oil is hot when it first flows from the well, it is cooled virtually to sea temperature when loaded. The hot spots on an imaging infra-red picture of a tanker are the funnel, ventilators and engine room, and it is these areas that have been repeatedly struck. The resulting damage has often been remarkably small, as has the casualty rate. When vessels have been hit in the tank spaces, fires have either not broken out at all or have been very small and quickly extinguished. However, when a weapon has struck engine room and accommodation, fire has often broken out. In a number of cases the spaces have been completely gutted, reducing the vessel to a constructive total loss. The *Al Ahood* burned for nine days after a missile passed through the settling tanks into the engine room, the fire then being oil-fed. Even then her whole cargo was saved before the vessel was declared a constructive total loss.

The highly automated *Safina al Arab* also became a constructive total loss because of the expense of repairing such a sophisticated vessel after an Exocet had caused extensive damage to her machinery and

The fire is out, revealing the extent of the structural collapse of *Al Ahood*'s stern and superstructure. The heat was so intense that normally sound structures became plastic and unable to support their own weight. The base of the pillar supporting the port bridge wing is compressed and the whole superstructure has settled into the hull of the ship. Similar structural collapse took place on the two British Type 21 frigates *Antelope* and *Ardent*, lost in the Falklands in 1982. (*Smit International*)

computers. Of her 350,000-ton cargo only some 10,000 tons were lost.

The low manning levels in these large vessels have meant that there have been comparatively few casualties. Engine-room staff have been vulnerable, however, the *Buyuk Hun*, *Fidelity*, *Al Ahood* and *Tiburon* all having lost all or part of their engine-room watches when struck by missiles.

The immediate effect of weapon impact has generally been small. The resulting fires have caused extensive damage, but when fire has not resulted the structural damage has usually been quickly repairable. In a number of cases the cost of the repair is likely to be less than that of the missile used to inflict the damage.

It was hoped that analysis of the incidents in the Persian Gulf would give some indication of the effectiveness of modern weapon systems against merchant ships and, coupled with study of the Falklands War, assist in both improving the weapons and devising protective measures. However, more questions have been raised than have been answered.

That small Western warships can be knocked out by a single hit from an air-to-surface weapon – even one that did not explode – and that they burn readily was demonstrated by the loss of *Sheffield*. It is not known whether the smaller ships of the Warsaw Pact would burn similarly, but the fire following an internal explosion in the Kashin-class destroyer *Otvazhny* in 1974 suggests that fire control in Soviet vessels may be little better than that of their British counterparts.

The terminal velocity, kinetic energy and explosive capacity of a missile like Exocet are equivalent to those of a single heavy shell. Experience in two world wars has shown that merchant ships and small warships are capable of absorbing multiple hits from heavy weapons. The use of modern weapons against large ships in the Persian Gulf has raised two questions which are fundamental to the defence of the Western maritime powers. Are the anti-ship missiles possessed by the West powerful enough to destroy or put out of action a major surface unit? Are the large carriers of the United States Navy really as vulnerable as their critics allege?

It has become clear that a single weapon with a medium-sized warhead does not necessarily cause seri-

Struck in the engine room, *Tiburon* settles by the stern and blazes fiercely. Eight men were killed and three injured in this attack. (*Smit International*)

Water is sprayed onto the deck of *Tiburon* to prevent over-heating of the crude oil cargo. (*Smit International*)

Portable pumps on the deck of the tug *Smit Colombo* play high-pressure water jets onto *Tiburon*'s superstructure. At this stage the spread of the fire had been controlled. (*Smit International*)

Once the *Tiburon* deck fire had been pushed back, salvage crews wearing close-quarters firefighting suits made a concerted foam attack on the conflagration in the enclosed spaces. The pump room was filled with foam to act as a fire barrier. In this picture excess foam runs over the deck as three members of the Dutch fire crew take a quick break. (*Smit International*)

After 120hr of day and night labour the fire on the Swiss-owned *Tiburon* is out. Tugs and crew await the arrival of the 35,000-ton *Kourion* to take off 25,000 tons of oil from the after tanks and bring the vessel onto an even keel. This done, the remaining cargo, worth $50 million, was transferred to the BP tanker *British Renown*, herself the victim of an attack while on her way to *Tiburon*. The badly damaged *Tiburon* was subsequently sold to Taiwanese shipbreakers after 99% of her cargo had been recovered. (*Smit International*)

ous damage to a large target, while one with a small warhead (or one that does not explode) can destroy a target if it hits vital or flammable areas. Unless the missile is deflected by countermeasures, radar terminal guidance causes it to impact in the centre of the radar image. In the case of an engines-aft merchant vessel, the centre of the radar image is generally a bare hull. The infra-red-homing weapons have struck the hot spots of the infra-red image: engine room, funnels, uptakes and ventilators, all vital, flammable areas. It should also be remembered that the exhaust gases from a gas-turbine-powered warship are hotter than those of the low-speed diesel engines of a large tanker or bulk carrier, and create a correspondingly brighter infra-red image.

Soviet air-to-surface and surface-to-surface missiles generally have much larger warheads than their Western equivalents, with explosive charges in the 1,000–2,200lb range. Is this a more realistic approach to anti-ship warfare?

We have now witnessed the effect of modern weapon systems on large merchant ships and small warships but have yet to see what they would do to major warships like the US Navy's carriers or the larger ships of the Soviet Navy. Judging from the damage-resistance of the ships attacked in the Persian Gulf, there seems little reason to doubt the survivability of a carrier such as USS *Nimitz*, with her 2,000 watertight compartments, if the fire hazard can be contained. Throughout the Second World War, from *Illustrious* in the Mediterranean to the US carrier groups in the Pacific, carriers demonstrated their ability to absorb punishment. This was underlined as recently as 1969, when nine 500lb bombs (equal to twelve Exocet warheads) exploded on the flight deck of USS *Enterprise* with results that, while not insignificant, were not disastrous.

The one lesson to be learned is that fire is the main danger to the survival of our ships. Every effort must be made in the design of new ships and the refit of existing units to increase fire resistance by means of improved vessel layout, the correct selection of materials and the provision of effective firefighting equipment.

Attacks on merchant ships in the Gulf

Date	Ship	Flag	Weapon	Damage	Casualties	Remarks
Before March 30, 1984	*Filikon L*	Greek	Exocet (unexploded)	Three frames and scupper pipe holed, together with bulkhead slop tank and No 4 wing tank	Nil	Weapon disarmed and dismantled by USN. 200 tons oil leaked. Hole 6in above waterline. No fires
April 18	*Rover Star*		Missile	In ballast, slight damage only, vessel able to continue loading	Nil	May 2: missile reported as Exocet. Repaired at Kharg Island
April 25	*Safina al Arab*	Saudi	Exocet	10,000 tons of cargo burned, 340,000 tons salvaged	Nil	Damage to machinery space, superstructure. Vessel highly automated. Cost of replacing machinery, hydraulics, steering gear and computers too high; ship declared constructive total loss
May 2	*Sea Eagle*	Liberian	Missile	"Minor"		Loaded bulk carrier; fertiliser absorbed force of impact
May 8	*Al Ahood*	Saudi	Missile		1	Missile passed through settling tanks into engine room. Extensive fires for 9 days; oil-fed fire due to cracked tank. Vessel declared constructive total loss in August. Cargo saved
May 13	*Umm Casbah*	Kuwaiti	"Projectile"	Confined to central tank, no fire		Vessel repaired by May 16
May 14	*Tabriz Esparanza II*	Iranian Greek				In ballast. Engine room and accommodation burned out
	Bahrah	Kuwaiti	2 missiles	Hit in Nos 4 and 5 wing tanks. Pump room fire extinguished by crew. Hole 5m². Also hit in accommodation.	2 injured	Dry-docked for repairs May 19

Date	Ship	Flag	Weapon	Damage	Casualties	Remarks
May 16	*Yanbu Pride*	Kuwaiti	Rocket or cannon after missile strike		Nil	Fire burned 3hr, extinguished with assistance of Saudi Coastguard. 5 rockets fired, 2 hit. Later strafed
May 18	*Fidelity*	Yugoslav crew	2 Exocet	Sunk	3 killed 3 injured	Bulk carrier loaded with steel
May 24	*Chemical Venture*	Liberian	1 "heat seeking rocket"	Wheelhouse burned out	6 injured	Machinery undamaged. In ballast. Vessel towed to Japan for repairs
May 31	*Atlanticos*	Liberian				Reports of hit denied by master
June 3	*Buyuk Hun*	Turkish	Exocet, Super Etendard-launched		3 dead, 2 injured	Two missiles hit port side, entering engine room. Watch killed. Vessel towed to Kharg Island and fire extinguished
June 5	*Savoy Dean*	Liberian	Missile	Slight	Nil	Bulk carrier carrying grain
June 10	*Kazimah*	?	Missile	Two tanks damaged	Nil	Ship in ballast. Small fire quickly extinguished. "Nine bombs missed before missile hit." Lloyds surveyor issued seaworthiness certificate and vessel sailed June 11
June 24	*Alexander the Great*	Greek	Missile (believed Exocet)	Small fire in No 5 port wing tank. 600 tons of steelwork to renew. Side buckled 20m, shell torn 10m × 2½m, deck buckled	Nil	Ship carrying "full cargo." Missile hit side, was deflected and did not explode
June 27	*Tiburon*	Swiss-operated	Heat-seeking missile	Fire throughout engine room and superstructure burned for 5 days. Aft end gutted	8 killed, 3 injured	Missile struck 1.5m above waterline, entering engine room
July 1	*Won Jin Alexandra Dyo*	Korean Panamanian. Greek-owned and manned	2 missiles		2 killed, 6 injured	Set on fire, total loss
July 5	*Primrose*	Liberian. Japanese crew	2 missiles	No 3 port aft tank indent 200 × 400 × 150mm. Internal machinery and fans damaged in engine room. Hole in hull 4m × 3m. No fire	Nil	6 rockets fired in two runs by F-4 Phantom. 1 missile struck deck, the other hit engine room casing
July 10	*British Renown*	British	2 rockets		Nil	Hit foremast and No 2 starboard tank. Little damage, small fire. One rocket bounced off deck, other tore away oil loading gear

Red Sea mines a mystery no longer

Capt John Moore RN

غات
طرابلس

GHAT
TRIPOLI

As state terrorism takes over from the operations of small groups, the warnings published in *Jane's Fighting Ships* and elsewhere over the last eight years have now proved only too well founded. These cautions concerned the feasibility of minelaying by terrorist organisations in ports and channels. The mine incidents in the Red Sea during July–September 1984 amply proved the effectiveness of such activity. Had these mines been laid in the approaches to a major port, the

clearance work would have been easier but the results even more damaging.

The first ship affected was the Soviet Ro-Ro vessel *Knud Jespersen*, which in the late evening of July 9 had just left the Suez Canal and was approaching the traffic

---

The Libyan Ro-Ro ship *Ghat*, the likely culprit in the Red Sea mining affair. (*Aquitaine Maritime Agencies*)

separation lanes to the southward, bound into the Red Sea. She was in less than 30m of water when an explosion "under the hull" resulted in her anchoring off Adabiya for inspection and repairs. This work was completed eight days later and she sailed on July 18, the victim of a single mysterious occurrence.

Thus it remained until at 1510 on July 27 the Liberian *Medi Sea* suffered a similar explosion, which stopped the main engines and brought the ship's electrics off the board. Shortly after she had once more got under way and made Suez, the Japanese *Meiyo Maru* set off another detonation only a few miles from the *Medi Sea* incident. She sustained only minor damage. At almost the same time the Panamanian general cargo ship *Este* had her engines stopped by an explosion off Ras Shukheir, some 90 miles to the southward.

By now it was obvious that mines of unknown characteristics had been laid in the area. On July 28 the small Panamanian vessel *Bigorange XII* suffered extensive damage in her engine room, the Spanish 77,604 GRT tanker *Valencia* set off another mine but suffered little apparent damage, and the Cypriot *Linera* was damaged off Ras Shukheir. This was the last of this group of mines to explode until on September 20 the Saudi Arabian Ro-Ro ship *Belkis I* of 3,114 GRT was slightly damaged some 30 miles south of Suez.

In the meantime the Egyptian Government had asked for help, and minehunters from the Royal Navy, France and Italy and MCM helicopters from the US Navy collaborated in a comprehensive search of the southern Suez exits. The first mine was discovered by a French ship: it turned out to be of Soviet origin, laid during the Arab–Israeli war in 1973. On September 17 it was announced that a second mine had been found, this time by a British minehunter. Lying in 40m of water 15 miles south of Suez, on the edge of the southbound lane, it was raised and transported into shallow water so that its firing mechanism could be dismantled. Those details available at the time of writing make it clear that it is a specimen of a comparatively modern Soviet bottom mine designed to be laid by submarine and embodying any or all of the non-contact methods of detonation – magnetic, acoustic and pressure. However, some reports from damaged ships suggest that it is in fact an acoustic mine, detonated by the beat of the ship's screws, and probably containing a reduced explosive charge. It would be possible to lay such mines from a surface ship, provided some adjustments were made.

Before the minehunters arrived at Suez the first two of ten explosions had taken place in the southern Red Sea on July 31. In the 20-mile-wide channel between Great Hanish Island and the coast of Yemen, about 75 miles in from the Straits of Bab el Mandeb, the Bahamian vessel *Peruvian Reefer* and the Chinese *Hui Yang* were damaged by separate explosions. In the latter case the mine was reported as detonating 30m to starboard.

On August 2 this field had a bumper harvest. In a 30-mile stretch the Greek *Kriti Coral*, the Turkish *Morgul*, the East German *Georg Schumann* and the North Korean *Dai Hong Dan*, all of between 5,000 and 12,000 GRT, suffered damage to their engines. The largest, the 11,849 GRT *Kriti Coral*, was in the shallowest part of the channel and reported that she was "lifted clear of the water, falling back with strong vibrations." Allowing for a measure of justifiable hyperbole, there was clearly a very big bang, which suggests something larger than a 600lb mine. On August 3 the Chinese container ship *Tang He* of 16,108 GRT was damaged by an explosion 80m away but was able to proceed after repairs.

The next day passed without incident, but on August 5 the Liberian tanker *Oceanic Energy* of 41,436 GRT was involved in the most extraordinary event of the series. At 0815, off the Farasan Bank and 185 miles east-south-east of Port Sudan, she reported that she had "struck a mine." This came as little surprise under the circumstances, but the position given was in 500m of water in one of the wider parts of the Red Sea. "A big explosion on the starboard side was followed by three or four smaller ones": these might have been the result of internal bulkheads collapsing, but even so the damage was considerable. Severe damage to the hull extended for 60m along the starboard side, there was a fire, which was quickly extinguished, and the ship took an angle by the bow. Most of the crew abandoned ship and one man was reported missing. The crew subsequently returned and the ship was towed to Jeddah, where she arrived on August 13 for survey. This incident immediately suggested the use of some form of floating mine, although the chances of collision between ship and mine must have been infinitesimal. Other possibilities include a US Captor-type weapon which can release a torpedo from a mine casing, or a straightforward submarine attack. Both appear equally unlikely, so the *Oceanic Energy* conundrum remains unsolved. However, the most likely cause is an internal explosion.

On August 6 the Soviet fish carrier *Bastion* of 633 GRT struck a mine; the damage was not reported. On August 11 the Polish *Jozef Wybicki* sustained damge to her engine-room piping and was brought to a temporary halt. Both ships were in the channel south-east of Great Hanish Island and eventually proceeded to their destinations. Another four days passed peacefully before the Cypriot cargo ship *Theoupolis* suffered hull damage and power failure after an explosion in the same channel on August 15. At the time of writing she was the last casualty in the southern area, in which the Soviet Navy carried out minesweeping operations for an undisclosed period. Casualty total in both the north and south fields was 18 by the end of September 1984, with one doubtful incident.

As the incidents were reaching a peak a group known

as Islamic Jihad claimed responsibility for laying 190 mines. Jihad had shown itself to be fanatical and effective in operations in the Lebanon and against other Middle Eastern targets, but maritime action, even the laying of mines, requires some form of professional backing. The organisation receives support from Iran, Syria and Libya, all countries with significant naval resources. Iran, although possessing no warships specifically equipped for minelaying, has for a long time held a stock of US mines which could be laid by specially converted aircraft or merchant ships.

For at least 11 years Libya has held a stock of mines which were delivered from an unknown source some time before Soviet naval transfers began. In June 1973 a couple of protective barriers were laid off the main Libyan ports, and today a number of surface ships and six ex-Soviet submarines are all fitted for minelaying. This implies not only a knowledge of this task but also a store of Soviet mines, including 21in-diameter types designed for tube-launching from submarines. Although the Syrian Navy is less advanced than the Libyan, it does include half a dozen ex-Soviet ships with a minelaying capability.

Thus all three countries which support Islamic Jihad have stocks of sea mines of diverse origins and capable of being laid by warships, submarines, aircraft or merchant ships. Neither aircraft nor military vessels have been reported in either mined area, with the result that suspicion has focused on merchant ships. Prime suspect is the Libyan Ro-Ro ship *Ghat*. The actual laying of a mine is unspectacular, the size of the splash varying only with the height from the rails to the sea. It is the fitting of these rails that rapidly converts a merchant ship into a minelayer. In the days before roll-on/roll-off ships, with their stern and side doors, apertures had to be cut in a ship's stern to allow the mines to be stowed in and laid from the interior of the ship. *Ghat* has both side and stern doors.

Early in July she left Leghorn bound for the Suez Canal. According to the Egyptian authorities, Lieutenant Zuheir Adham of the Libyan mine-warfare division and a Libyan colonel, Sadeq Balfel, were embarked and the crew changed before *Ghat* made the Canal transit. On July 10 she anchored off Assab, having made her passage at an average speed of about 12kt. She remained off Ethiopia's main port until July 14, when she berthed alongside, sailing on July 17 for Suez. The main shipping route is to the east of Great Hanish Island. Such are the problems of shore-fixing inherent in any Red Sea passage, this is the obvious choice for any prudent mariner who doesn't want to leave his keel on the Muhabbaka reefs or the Haycocks. The northward voyage took longer than the outward trip, the speed made good being more in the region of 10kt. *Ghat* transited the Canal on July 22 and proceeded to Tripoli and thence to Southern France. Her cargo was not examined during either Canal transit,

and a French customs search revealed nothing unusual.

If *Ghat* were the culprit the dates would fit remarkably well. The first casualty off Suez occurred three days after *Ghat* went south. A time delay can be fitted to any mine, and this casualty may have resulted from the malfunction of one of these devices. The next explosions occurred five days after *Ghat* had passed northbound. The first two in the southern group came four days later. Thus if *Ghat* were responsible, a time delay of three weeks for the Suez field and two weeks for the southern field would not only have ensured her safe return passage but would also have given her operators time to reach Tripoli, unrig her mine rails and other impedimenta, apply a lick of paint and turn her once more into an innocuous merchant ship. Whatever the type of mine in use, this timetable remains applicable.

All the above is circumstantial evidence which can be summarised briefly. *Ghat*, belonging to Libya, a country known to support the terrorist group claiming to have laid 190 mines in the Red Sea, arrives at Port Said, changes her crew, embarks a senior officer and a mining expert, and transits the Canal bound for Assab. Three days later a ship is sunk, presumably by a mine, off Suez. Two weeks after *Ghat* sails for Suez from Assab, the first of ten ships is damaged by a mine in a passage most probably used by *Ghat*. Five days after *Ghat* clears the Canal bound for Tripoli, the first of seven ships is mined in the approaches to Suez. The one mine recovered is of Soviet origin, and is of the type that was probably supplied for the Libyan submarines.

These developments were followed by expressions of delight from the Iranian Foreign Minister which were hastily disavowed by the Ayatollah Khomeini. However, the latter soon received a telex message from President Gaddafi of Libya: "Pleased and content for the work accomplished in the Red Sea." And in December 1984 the two officers and new crew of *Ghat* were all decorated for their services.

If the figure of 190 mines laid is accurate, the striking rate of one ship per ten mines must stand as a record. So far, however, this is an almost unique case. It is the first time – except for the Albanian incident in 1951, the mining of Haiphong harbour in 1972 and the recent Nicaraguan campaign – that waterways in general use have been mined in conditions short of a major and widespread war. Targets of the Albanian action were British warships, while the Haiphong mining was given publicity, as required by international law. Similarly, the Nicaraguan operation, though heavily criticised, had a clearly stated objective. In the Red Sea no warning was given and the sufferers, sailing under 14 different flags, had a wide range of political affiliations. The fact that only minor damage resulted might be due to a deliberate decision to do no more than intimidate ship operators. But it would surprise no one if the perpetrators of this typically callous attack subsequently took their campaign a lethal step further.

Ships damaged by mines in the Red Sea, July–September 1984

Date	Ship and flag	GRT	Depth of water (m)	Area (north/south)
July 9	*Knud Jespersen* (USSR)	8,815	under 30	N
July 27	*Medi Sea* (Liberia)	14,136	55	N
July 27	*Meiyo Maru* (Japan)	17,380	50	N
July 27	*Este* (Panama)	4,627	40	N
July 28	*Bigorange XII* (Panama)	846	under 30	N
July 28	*Valencia* (Spain)	77,604	42	N
July 28	*Linera* (Cyprus)	9,498	40	N
July 31	*Peruvian Reefer* (Bahamas)	6,010	50	S
July 31	*Hui Yang* (China)	9,913	45	S
Aug 2	*Kriti Coral* (Greece)	11,849	50	S
Aug 2	*Morgul* (Turkey)	5,150	50	S
Aug 2	*Georg Schumann* (E. Germany)	7,723	33	S
Aug 2	*Dai Hong Dan* (N. Korea)	6,608	50	S
Aug 3	*Tang He* (China)	16,108	35	S
Aug 6	*Bastion* (USSR)	633	38	S
Aug 11	*Josef Wybicki* (Poland)	8,644	35	S
Aug 15	*Theoupolis* (Cyprus)	11,765	35	S
Sep 20	*Belkis I* (Saudi Arabia)	3,114	50	N

Damage to *Ocean Energy* (Liberia) on August 5 is more likely to have been due to an internal explosion.

NATO's naval commanders face perennial problems

Adm Sir James Eberle

Some years ago it was reported that General Bernard Rogers, the Supreme Commander Europe (SACEUR), when discussing with his staff some naval business put forward by the two other major NATO commanders (MNCs), the Supreme Commander Atlantic (SAC-LANT) and the Commander-in-Chief Channel (CIN-CHAN), said: "What's all this about there being two naval MNCs – there are three naval MNCs!" This story reflects an aspect of NATO's maritime posture that is all too often forgotten: national naval forces are assigned to all three NATO supreme commanders, with the result that SACEUR controls the sizeable Allied naval forces in the Mediterranean, the Baltic and its approaches, and the narrow coastal waters of Norway. There are therefore in effect a number of separate NATO fleets, just as there are separate Soviet fleets.

General Rogers' remark also perhaps indicates the difficulties of maintaining in the staff of SHAPE (Supreme Headquarters Allied Powers Europe), which is principally concerned with the land battle, enough senior maritime expertise to handle naval activities ranging from inshore fast patrol boat work in the Norwegian fiords to open-water aircraft carrier operations in the Ionian Sea.

The Soviet Union's formidable amphibious warfare capability would be sure to present the NATO command structure with severe problems. Here one armoured personnel carrier swims away from an Alligator-class LST as another enters the water from the bow ramp. (*Novosti*)

The division of NATO's naval forces between different commanders gives rise to great complexities of operational command and control. Many of these arise from the need for geographical boundaries between the various commands. This problem is particularly acute in the North Sea adjacent to the Baltic Approaches. Attempts to overcome the difficulties by changing the boundaries have not been successful, prompting a switch to procedures which promote maximum flexibility in cross-boundary operations. Such co-operation between the Atlantic and Channel commands is greatly assisted by the arrangement under which CINCHAN, a major NATO commander in his own right, is also subordinated to SACLANT as CINCEASTLANT.

The closest possible maritime co-operation between three major NATO commanders is vital to the success of the alliance's strategy in both peace and war. Fortunately, the days are past when it could be said that SACEUR and SACLANT were preparing to fight two different wars. Nevertheless, there still exists a certain underlying tension which manifests itself in occasional strong statements from senior naval commanders to the effect that their resources are inadequate for the task, and that the alliance devotes too much of its attention to the Central Front and not enough to the flanks and the situation at sea. Of course, it can also be said that there is an imbalance of forces on the Central Front. But while in land warfare a successful assault requires a large superiority of attackers over defenders, in naval warfare it is the opposite which applies. The advantage at sea lies with the attacker, not the defender.

Underlying the debate about the validity of NATO's strategy is the "short war/long war" argument. There are those who argue that NATO's in-place forces in Central Europe could hold a full-scale Soviet attack for only a small number of days before it would be necessary for the military commanders to request the use of nuclear weapons. Thereafter, nuclear escalation would be swift and seaborne reinforcements from the USA would arrive too late to affect significantly the ground situation. Thus naval operations in the Atlantic, other than those connected with SSBNs, would be largely irrelevant to the outcome of the war. The naval protagonists argue that, without the assurance of seaborne reinforcement and resupply, the credibility of the strategy of flexible response would be seriously weakened and deterrence undermined. Furthermore, they point out that the choice of whether a war, however it breaks out, is of short or long duration does not rest with the defenders, and that NATO planning for a short war only would amount to a direct invitation to the Warsaw Pact to plan for a long one.

The concepts on which NATO maritime operations are based have been re-examined in depth in an effort to improve the coherence of the alliance's naval planning and relate it to the overall strategy. This study included an examination of the need for forward defence at sea as well as on the Central Front; the problems of preventing the Soviets from maintaining the strategic or tactical initiative, despite the fact that NATO would never strike the first blow; and the security of seaborne supplies of energy and raw materials through NATO's vulnerable "economic flank." Although this work did much to provide a basis for common naval planning by the staffs of the three MNCs, it did not resolve the apparent contradiction between the needs of maritime operations in the Atlantic and those of ground operations on the Central Front. Indeed, such contradiction is inherent in the uncertainty which is an integral part of the strategy of deterrence. However, it would not occur in a strategy for the conduct of war itself, should deterrence fail. The differences in a strategy for avoiding war and one for conducting war are perhaps insufficiently understood. The latter must take into account the circumstances in which fighting has broken out, the former cannot.

The only certainty about the circumstances in which hostilities might start is that many of them will be unexpected. Nevertheless, certain major naval options are clearly evident. The Soviets would have to decide what proportion of their 260-strong attack submarine force to deploy into the deep Atlantic against reinforcement and resupply (RE/RE) shipping, and whether to devote more resources to the RE/RE shipping than to the NATO strike fleet. In other words, would this large force, which includes an increasing percentage of nuclear-propelled boats of improving quality, go for NATO's warships or its merchantmen? There is also the major problem of how the Soviets should deploy their surface ships from the Northern Fleet. Should they deploy them before the outbreak of hostilities in the Eastern Atlantic? If so, how to ensure their subsequent survival? (A similar problem of post-initial exchange survival exists for Soviet surface ships in the Mediterranean.) Or should they hold them back in Northern waters for subsequent operations in the Norwegian Sea? The increasing size and defensive capability of the newer surface ships, such as the *Kirov* and *Slava* classes and in due course the new fixed-wing aircraft carrier, provide, in theory at least, a wider range of options for the Soviet Naval Command, while their offensive capability represents a significant increase in threat.

The NATO commanders face not dissimilar choices. What proportion of the NATO submarine force should be pushed forward into Northern waters? And how should the aircraft carriers of the NATO strike fleet be initially deployed? In the Atlantic in direct or indirect support of RE/RE shipping, or forward through the GIUK Gap into the Norwegian Sea? From there they could put pressure on the Soviet Northern Fleet bases and provide air support for ground operations in North Norway; though only at increasing risk from shore-based, missile-armed Backfire strike aircraft.

Though Supreme Headquarters Allied Powers Europe is principally concerned with land operations it also has to maintain enough naval expertise to handle units ranging from this Norwegian torpedo boat to a full-scale carrier battle group. (*L. & L. van Ginderen*)

A fundamental uncertainty facing the naval commanders on both sides concerns the vulnerability of the large ships of the battle groups to SSN torpedo or missile attack. Second World War experience is of little value here because the submarines of that day were too slow. Exercise results are, for various and complex reasons, of doubtful validity. The Falklands War gives us few reliable clues, other than that the Argentinian cruiser *General Belgrano* was found and sunk by an SSN using Second World War-type torpedoes. The Argentinian carrier *Veinticinco de Mayo* was not found, while a probable Argentinian conventional submarine attack on *Invincible* was not successful. This level of uncertainty would be likely, at least initially, to lead to the cautious use of major surface units.

Another major area of concern to NATO commanders is the likely shortage of escorts for the protection of RE/RE shipping. The increasing size, complexity and cost of frigate-type ships has led to serious reductions in their numbers, to the extent that there might well not be enough escort forces available to permit the convoying of merchant ships should this be necessary. There continues to be doubt about the effectiveness of convoying in the face of modern submarine, reconnaissance and weapon capabilities, and alternative defensive concepts, such as defended lanes, have been developed. But although the SSN and maritime patrol aircraft are highly effective tools of modern anti-submarine warfare, the failure of Western navies to design an effective ocean escort that is cheap enough to be produced in relatively large numbers places severe limitations on NATO's ability to protect its sea lines of communication.

The problem of transatlantic resupply is aggravated by the recent severe reductions in Western merchant fleets. Although the requirement for military reinforcement is clearly and closely defined, and can still be met, the amount of shipping needed for military and civil resupply is harder to assess. The Falklands experience has also shown how valuable certain specialised merchant ships can be in direct support of military operations. These two latter requirements, together with the need to replace war losses, give rise to fears that a further uncontrolled reduction in the numbers of Western merchant ships, nationally crewed and sailing under their own flags, could have serious military consequences.

Transatlantic resupply is also jeopardised by the threat to the European reception ports, particularly by mining. The potential of this form of warfare has been most recently underlined by the covert laying of mines in the Red Sea. Such a campaign, carried out in European waters before the outbreak of hostilities, could stretch NATO's mine countermeasures forces to the limit.

Against this background of shortages in almost all categories, the NATO naval commanders are hard put to answer when asked by the political authorities: "Can you nevertheless still accomplish your tasks?" For many reasons it is difficult to justify either a simple "Yes" or "No." The commander therefore tends to reply: "Yes but . . ." The "buts" will be real and very important to him, but all too often the politician will forget them or dismiss them as military over-caution. It was this situation that during the 1970s led one of the most distinguished and respected Supreme Commanders Atlantic to declare that in view of the deteriorating naval balance he could no longer carry out all his mission at the same time. The tasks would in future have to be undertaken in sequence, resulting in very difficult decisions on priorities. Although this stratagem drew attention to the worsening balance of maritime forces, it has not been successful, except in the United States, as a means of obtaining more money for navies. Rather has it been used as an excuse for politicians, faced with an ever-increasing mismatch between requirements and available reserves, to reduce the priority of naval missions and thus justify a reduction in naval programmes. The extreme example of this was the British Government's proposal for naval cuts just before the Falklands War. As another senior NATO naval commander put it: "It is not unreasonable to expect us to get better value from what we have now – but we cannot reasonably be expected to get more out of less."

The major problems confronting NATO naval commanders today are essentially little different from those that have faced British naval commanders through the ages: how best to combine sea and land power in a coherent strategy for the security of Europe; the difficulties of maintaining an effective system of command and control without losing operational flexibility; and a shortage of ships of all kinds. These problems cannot be solved by high technology alone. Their solution lies ultimately in the professional skill of naval leaders and the willingness of governments to expand the resources needed to prevent the Soviet Union from achieving maritime superiority in sea areas vital to the security of the NATO alliance.

The Allied transatlantic resupply effort, as typified by this British-registered self-sustaining cargo vessel, would be gravely threatened by the Soviet Navy's 260-boat attack submarine fleet. (*Skyfotos*)

Norway: key to the North Atlantic

Commodore Harald Ronneberg RNN

When NATO was born and the military organisation decided upon, Norway, together with Denmark and the northern part of West Germany, became the Major Subordinate Command, Allied Forces Northern Europe, under the Supreme Commander Allied Forces Europe (SACEUR). But even at that time Norwegian naval officers believed that Norway, because of its geographical position, should be a SACLANT (Supreme Allied Commander Atlantic) responsibility. In their opinion Norway was more an eastern flank for SACLANT than a northern flank for SACEUR. Be that as it may, there can be no doubting the strategic importance of Northern Norway to NATO as a whole.

The fact that the German occupation of Norway very nearly cut the vital supply lines between North America, the United Kingdom and the USSR today makes the Soviet leaders doubly aware of the strategic importance of Norway and, in particular, Northern Norway. It should also be remembered that Norway has borders of some 106km with the USSR, 716km with Finland (signatory of a non-aggression treaty with the USSR), and 1,643km with neutral Sweden. Nor should NATO ignore the strategic value of the Finnish Wedge, where the Germans and Finns built a road usable by heavy armour thrusting towards the northernmost part of the Troms area, with its all-important army, air force and naval bases. Whoever controls Northern Norway can also control the transatlantic reinforcement and supply lines.

Trondheim, launched in 1963, is one of the five 1,745-ton *Oslo*-class frigates. Forming part of the programme approved in 1960, they were all built in Norway, with half the cost being borne by the USA. The design is basically that of the USN *Dealey*-class DEs, modified to meet Norwegian requirements. (*L. & L. van Ginderen*)

The Soviet Navy is divided into four fleets: the Pacific, the Black Sea and Mediterranean, the Baltic and the Northern. The Northern Fleet, based on the Kola Peninsula, currently presents the greatest threat to NATO. It will become even more of a danger if it can shift its bases westwards into Northern Norway.

The first C-in-C North was Admiral Sir Patrick Brind (1951–53); apparently the problems of defending NATO's northern flank at that time were mostly maritime. The successors have all been generals, but they too recognised the importance of keeping Northern Norway under NATO command and control. From bases in this area NATO can cover the exits from the Barents Sea between the Arctic icecap and the Svalbard island group to the north and North Cape and Finnmark to the south. Svalbard, along with the Bear Island group and Jan Mayen away to the west, are Norwegian sovereign territory. But in accordance with the treaty of 1924 which ceded Svalbard to Norway, the establishment of any form of military establishment or fortification on the islands is prohibited. Jan Mayen is however an important part of the NATO warning, surveillance and communications systems, to which Norway has contributed since the early years of the alliance.

The Soviet threat

A comparison of current Northern Fleet naval and maritime air forces with the Soviet Navy of the Second World War makes disturbing reading. At the time of the German attack in 1941 the Soviet Navy consisted of three very antiquated battleships, three new cruisers of the *Kirov* class, and three older cruisers. Fifty destroyers were completed during the latter part of the 1930s, and there were 15 more of pre-First World War vintage. The Soviets had a large submarine fleet of

The 780-ton corvette *Sleipner* (illustrated), her sister *Aeger* and the *Oslo* class make up the main surface ship strength of the Royal Norwegian Navy. The primary arms of the fleet are the 14 Type 207 submarines and about 50 fast attack and patrol craft.

about 200 boats. During the war the Western Allies lent the USSR HMS *Royal Sovereign*, of about the same age as the three old Tsarist battleships, the US cruiser *Milwaukee* and nine of the 50 four-stackers that President Roosevelt transferred to the Royal Navy under the Anglo-American Agreement of September 2, 1940. Along with three more *Kirov*-class cruisers completed during the war, this was the sum total of major Soviet Navy warships in the Pacific, the Black Sea, the Baltic and the Northern fleets.

Today the Northern Fleet has 45 strategic missile submarines, 36 cruise missile submarines, 92 patrol submarines, two aircraft carriers, one battle-cruiser, 12 cruisers with various forms of missiles and gunnery and including two modified *Sverdlovs* from the 1950s, 19 destroyers and 47 frigates. The Baltic Fleet, which must also be considered a serious threat to SACEUR's northern flank, includes six strategic missile submarines, five cruise missile submarines, 25 patrol submarines, three cruisers and 40 destroyers/frigates.

The Northern Fleet includes 13 amphibious ships and craft, and the Baltic Fleet 53, of which 22 are air-cushioned vehicles. These naval forces are backed

One of the *Storm*-class fast attack craft, armed with six Penguin missiles, one 76mm gun and a 40mm, and capable of 32kt. All 20 of this class were built in Norway.

by significant air forces as well as missiles of various kinds on the Kola Peninsula and in other parts of the Soviet Union close to Norway, Finland and Sweden.

The politicians

This overwhelming maritime threat to NATO's flanks in the north and north-east is all the more serious because Western politicians appear to believe that the Soviets will not employ these forces against NATO. But why then have they spent so much of their gross national product on building up a clearly offensive force if they do not have the strategic aim of severing the North American supply lines to Continental Europe and the UK? I believe that this attitude is a great threat to the freedom of NATO's citizens, which those same politicians have been elected to protect.

Some years ago Norwegian border patrols in South Varanger witnessed a sizeable armoured spearhead thrusting towards the USSR–Norway border. The Norwegians were armed only with rifles, and they must have wondered whether this was the beginning of the end. Luckily their superiors kept their nerve and ordered no precipitate response, but to this day no-one can identify for certain the Soviet intention behind this demonstration of power. Was it to test the Norwegian speed of response in this area? A local military exercise? Or a purely political manoeuvre? The questions are many and in the main unanswered. But the incident does however illustrate that, despite satellite surveillance and NATO's various systems of warning and control, a surprise attack could be launched against the northern flank in Europe. Only political determination to demonstrate that this part of NATO is vital and must at all costs remain Norwegian can restrain the Kremlin from an adventure.

As for Norwegian politicians, I remember only too well how, with only a few exceptions, they betrayed Norway in 1940 through wishful thinking and a readiness to hide their heads in the sand.

The importance of Norwegian independence

The former Chief of Naval Staff and First Sea Lord, Admiral of the Fleet Sir Henry Leach, told me in September 1980 that the Allied lines of communication across the Atlantic could be maintained only by desperate efforts. Once they were lost, it would require even more desperate efforts to re-establish them. Since then the situation has deteriorated: our ships are older and fewer, and the Soviet naval, ground and air threat

Geir of the 14-strong *Hauk* class, all completed between 1977 and 1980. In addition to their six Penguin missiles and single 40mm and 20mm guns, they carry two torpedo tubes either side of the forecastle. Built at the same yards as the *Storm* class, they have a range of 440nm at their maximum speed of 34kt and carry a new weapon control system developed by Kongsberg.

Like all other NATO navies, that of Norway allowed its mine countermeasures forces to reach old age without replacement. *Sira* is one of a class of ten coastal minesweepers, half built in Norway and half in the USA. Now 30 years old, they comprise the entire mine-clearance capability of the RNN. (*Gilbert Gyssels*)

The 2,500-ton *Horten* was completed in 1978 as a depot ship for both submarines and fast attack craft. Norway's minimal coastal facilities, widely spaced ports and small population in the northern fjords meant that this form of support was urgently needed.

against the northern and north-eastern flank is more formidable than ever.

Even more disturbing is the fact that when senior officers voice their fears there is a tendency amongst the politicians to say that the defence chiefs intentionally overstate the military threat in an effort to keep their budgets high. This is happening in a country which as

recently as 1940 was overrun and occupied by a ruthless enemy because the defending forces were utterly inadequate. This time, however, it is not just a question of Norway's independence but of that of all the nations belonging to the NATO alliance.

The naval and air bases in Northern Norway are the keys to the defence of the reinforcement and supply lines across the North Atlantic. If these lines are not

Displacing only 100 tons, *Vernøy* is equipped not only for her primary role of torpedo recovery but also for firefighting and oil pollution clearance. She is an excellent example of maximum cost-effectiveness.

Norge, the Norwegian royal yacht, has the longest and most remarkable history of any ship in the RNN. In 1937 she was completed to the order of Mr T. O. M. Sopwith as an escort for his Americas Cup challengers *Endeavour I* and *II*. During the Second World War she retained her name of *Philante* and was well known to many naval people in the British Western Approaches Command. After the war the people of Norway bought her as a gift for King Haakon.

secure, the Allied forces under SACEUR will have little chance of standing up to Warsaw Pact aggression in Central and Southern Europe. Adequate defence of Northern Norway can only be achieved with the assistance of the forces of allied nations.

Norway's own forces in the north consist of one infantry battalion of 450 men in the Kirkenes area and a battalion group of about 1,000 men in Porsanger to the north-west. The Brigade North, with some 5,000 men, is based in the neighbouring county of Troms, and the ground forces are defended on their sea flank by some 15 coastal artillery fortifications, torpedo batteries and minefields.

The Royal Norwegian Navy has submarines and missile/gun/torpedo boats stationed in Northern Norway. Minelayers and amphibious craft are also available, and for most of the year there are also a couple of frigates stationed there.

The Royal Norwegian Air Force is based at five very important airfields. Air defence of these fields is totally inadequate, amounting to nothing more than a number of L.70 40mm cannon and 12.7mm machine guns. Infantry backed by tanks are also deployed for airfield defence.

Two F-16 fighter squadrons are permanently based in Northern Norway, and one squadron of P-3B Orion maritime patrol aircraft is based at Andenes. One more

squadron of F-16s and one with F-5s may be deployed from Southern Norway at short notice. However, Allied forces exercising with Norwegian units never enter Finnmark, a restriction imposed by Norway in an effort not to irritate her neighbour to the east.

Though the Norwegian Army has pre-stocked some heavy equipment in Troms, the only Allied stocks are held in the Trondheim area and even they are not yet complete. This equipment, destined for the US Marine Corps, is held in temporary stores while permanent structures are being built. When the plans for the pre-storing of Allied equipment were first prepared it was the Troms area that was of principal interest to the military commanders. The Norwegian Labour government was initially in agreement but later decided that it would be a provocation to the Soviets.

It is to be hoped that the standing forces listed here would be sufficient to defend the northern flank until

In April 1977 the Norwegian Coastguard was set up under the operational control of the Defence Command. *Farm* (W301) was built in 1962 and modernised soon after her transfer to the Coastguard. She and *Nornen* (W300) are typical of the 13 ships of the Coastguard, whose primary duties are fishery protection and oil rig patrol.

reinforcements reached this weak link in the NATO defence system. It is however up to the Norwegian Government to make a timely recommendation to the Storting (Parliament) that such aid should be asked for, and this decision is vital to the denial of Northern Norway to the Soviets.

Once under wartime Allied control, the bases in this region would cause the Soviet naval forces based on Kola great difficulties as they tried to reach the Atlantic. It is also to be hoped that SACLANT has his contingency plans for the defence of Svalbard and Jan Mayen up to date, as these are both outside SACEUR's zone of responsibility. Should a conflict start, both Soviet and NATO forces would surely hurry to fill the vacuum that currently exists in this very vulnerable area.

The French Navy in the year 2000

Pierre Lachamade

It's November 1961 and the French Navy's Mediterranean Squadron is sailing on exercise from Toulon. Two aircraft carriers and a pair of cruisers make for the open sea, attended by scores of brand-new *escorteurs d'escadre* and *escorteurs rapides* and covered from the air by the equally new Sikorsky helicopters. What a breathtaking sight for a midshipman on his first posting at sea. At Brest, *Clemenceau* is testing her catapults while the helicopter carrier *Jeanne d'Arc* – or rather *La Résolue*, as she is known while the old training cruiser still soldiers on – is being completed at the DCAN fitting-out pier.

Now move forward 23 years to 1984. *Jeanne d'Arc* has trained many hundreds of cadets over the last two decades and more, but her ops room still has the same radars and equipment, a long-delayed modernisation having been postponed for yet another year. The aircraft carriers still have over ten years' service ahead of them, while some of the destroyers, following very successful modernisations, are still fully operational.

Their successors are far more sophisticated – and far less numerous.

The 1961 midshipman, now a commander, must be wondering what the future holds for his service. Come the year 2000, will France have little more than a third-rate navy, a result of the decline that he has witnessed over the last 20 years? Or is the *Marine Nationale* about to undergo a renaissance that will assure it of a place amongst the West's leading navies?

1984, a year which saw another Le Bourget naval exhibition and the first months of the 1984–88 *Loi de Programmation Navale* (Naval Acquisition Programme), was a good time to consider the current situation and the prospects for the coming years.

The first French nuclear attack submarines were provided for in the 1974 estimates. These boats, of which S601 *Rubis* was the first, are the smallest operational nuclear submarines ever built. This was achieved in part by the use of liquid metal cooling. (*Giorgio Arra*)

The political background

Since May 1981 France has had a socialist government after several decades of Gaullist or post-Gaullist administration. This change, which made itself felt throughout French life, also had an impact on defence, though not as strongly as originally thought. With many reforms on its hands, a deteriorating economic situation, and the electorate becoming disenchanted after its initial enthusiasm, the Government has tried to keep its defence policy in line with its election commitments, particularly in the fields of foreign policy and finance without completely renouncing its traditional principles.

These objectives have proved hard to reconcile, but the following concrete developments have emerged:

• A renewed commitment to a French national deterrent, based mainly on the fleet ballistic submarines (SNLE).
• Confirmation of bilateral defence agreements with former French possessions in Africa.
• Expressions of interest in geographic areas outside France's usual sphere of influence.
• A cautious but nevertheless determined move closer to the Western Alliance after the touchy years of Gaullist independence, while still remaining outside the NATO military command structure in an effort to avoid any reduction in the French services' fighting capabilities.

The Government's determination to keep the armed forces at a high pitch of efficiency has been expressed in the *Loi de Programmation Militaire*, which defines the missions of the services up to the end of the century and promises the means to carry them out. Although past experience shows that naval programmes on such lines have seldom been fulfilled, usually as a result of unforeseen external factors, the *Loi de Programmation* remains a reasonable basis for prediction.

Three major programmes – a pair of nuclear-powered carriers, a new maritime patrol aircraft, and a class of amphibious landing ships – are due to get under way in 1984–88, while earlier programmes (nuclear attack submarines and various surface units) are continued. With an anticipated life of 25–30 years, including a mid-life weapon system update, these vessels will serve well into the 21st century. In the meantime, today's French Navy has been busy discharging commitments in a number of theatres.

Tied by the last government's defence agreements, France found itself deeply involved in Chad, countering a Libyan-backed rebel movement. French Navy participation amounted to two Atlantic maritime patrol aircraft on detachment. The explosive Indian Ocean situation, especially in the Gulf, has resulted in a continuous French Navy presence in the form of the ALINDIEN command. Created some 10 years ago, this significant force comprises destroyers, frigates and logistics vessels, occasionally reinforced by extra units from home, and is tasked with the protection of French tanker traffic in the Straits of Hormuz.

But the most striking feature of recent years has been the French involvement in the Middle East. As France tried to interpose itself between the fighting parties, from June 1982 to March 1984 the French Navy maintained 50,000 to 96,000 tons off Lebanon for the purpose of naval and air support and casualty evacuation. The force typically comprised an aircraft carrier, a missile frigate, a C 70 anti-submarine destroyer, two A 69 light frigates, a fleet replenishment tanker, an LPD, an LST, two LCTs and a civilian tanker, manned by a total of 3,500 men. This effort resulted in

Le Foudroyant, third of a class of five 8,940-ton ballistic missile submarines with nuclear propulsion, became operational in 1974. The entire design, including the weapons and all the internal systems, is of French origin. *L'Inflexible*, first of a new series, becomes operational in 1985. (*L. & L. van Ginderen*)

delayed overhauls for some vessels, and by July 1984 the Toulon dry docks and repair piers were unusually busy. Another consequence was reduced French participation in Allied exercises during 1984.

Although France withdrew from the NATO integrated command in 1966, significant links have been maintained or even improved. With liaison officers on all Allied staffs, France has remained more squarely than ever in the Western camp, as affirmed by Defence Minister Charles Hernu in 1983: "France is and will remain a loyal and consistent partner within the NATO alliance." Even if the French armed forces have developed their own organisation, tactics and weapons, they are nevertheless trained to operate with NATO forces.

In addition, frequent meetings at sea with Soviet naval ships, especially in the Mediterranean or the Indian Ocean, act as a constant reminder that the threat is close at hand. Increased Soviet activity and the fact that half of France's oil imports transit via Marseilles, prompted the French naval command to strengthen the Mediterranean Fleet. It now consists of some 14 combatant vessels manned by 6,000 men and totalling more than 100,000 tons. Included in the fleet are the two aircraft carriers, five new anti-submarine destroyers, an AOR, logistics vessels and some 12 attack submarines, including *Rubis* and *Saphir*, the new nuclear attack boats.

Another French commitment is the support of Iraq in the endless war against Iran. This has taken the form of huge sales of military hardware, particularly Exocet anti-ship missiles. These weapons have been fired from Super Frelon helicopters or ex-French Navy Super Etendards lent, leased or, possibly donated by the French Government. Only if Iraq wins – or, at least, does not lose – can the bill for this aid be paid, probably in oil.

Georges Leygues **was the first of seven Type C 70 ASW ships, the last of which is due to commission in 1989. Displacing 4,170 tons, these CODOG-propelled ships carry two Lynx helicopters, four Exocets, a Crotale SAM launcher and a single 100mm gun. Their diesels give a range of 9,500 miles at 18kt. (***Giorgio Arra***)**

The French Navy's missions

Now a medium-ranking power, France has nevertheless tried to maintain a measure of economic and military independence, resulting in air and naval capabilities second only to those of the superpowers. The primary mission of these forces is the defence of France, based on the principle of nuclear deterrence stated under General de Gaulle during the 1960s and reaffirmed by succeeding governments. The naval contribution comprises the ballistic missiles (16 per boat) of the six SNLEs (*Sousmarin Nucléaire Lance-Engins*) of the *Force Océanique Stratégique* (FOST).

Other Navy missions include a contribution to the defence of Western Europe within NATO; support of French interests worldwide, especially in the South Pacific, Indian Ocean and West Indies; protection of the merchant navy (1,199 vessels, 11,455,033 gross registered tons in 1984); support of French forces in operations to assist countries to which France is bound by military agreements; and control of a huge Exclusive Economic Zone (10 million square kilometres, third largest in the world). These missions have been confirmed in the *Loi de Programmation*, but can France afford the necessary ships and equipment?

1984 French Navy budget

As it is the first under the new five-year plan, the 1984 budget gives a good idea of what might be expected over the next few years. During the 1984 fiscal year some Fr12,092 million was to be spent on naval operations (up 4.42% on 1983) and Fr13,877 million on new construction (+12.83%), while a further Fr18,400 million for subsequent new building (+24.78%) was authorised. A number of points emerge from these bald figures:

• FOST's share of available funding increased from 14.36% to 16%, and its share of the authorisation from 29.9% to 35.04%.

• The naval air arm's share of available funding increased by 12.3%, and its share of the authorisation for aircraft procurement by fully 63.5%.

But there are matters of concern:

• The 3.6% decrease in funding for conventional new building.

• Increase in funding for fleet maintenance limited to 4.6%, which is sure to affect operational readiness.

• An 8.2% cut in spending on fuel (which accounts for no more than 3% of overall expenses), with corresponding unfortunate consequences for training. If the current level of activity is to be maintained, the Navy will have to draw on stocks built up in 1982–83.

Primary source of the extra money for the strategic and air arms is the navy's vital but unglamorous infrastructure. A reduction of numbers in all personnel categories (1,650 in 1983, 550 more in 1984) was made possible by a reorganisation of training establishments and by the fact that vessels being decommissioned outnumbered those entering service. Although base protection and refit facilities at Brest and Toulon are to be improved, the Direction des Constructions Armées

Clemenceau was commissioned in 1961, two years before her sister *Foch*. In 1978 she underwent a major refit to equip her to handle Super Etendard aircraft. She has a capacity of about 40 aircraft and is due to remain in service until 1995, by which time the first of two (planned) nuclear-propelled carriers is expected to be in commission. (*Giorgio Arra*)

Navales (DCAN) dockyards face cutbacks, with resulting consequences for local subcontractors. Man-hours worked at the dockyards were due to decline from 1981's 33 million to 29.2 million in 1984. Austerity measures in 1983 included a 25% increase in time between overhauls and a 12% reduction in expenditure on DCAN vessels and shore establishments. However, 70% of spending by the dockyards goes on wages, and this cannot be reduced without serious consequences for local employment. The early retirement of some ships can therefore be expected, as well as delays in refits.

All this was disquieting enough, but by mid-1984 the deteriorating economic situation and the new austerity measures expected with the arrival of Laurent Fabius as Prime Minister suggested that worse might be to come. In July 1984 President Mitterand indicated that in 1985 defence spending might be trimmed from the 1984 level of Fr171 billion, which represented a 7.7% rise over 1983. Though this was denied by Defence Minister Hernu – "The *Loi de Programmation Militaire* currently being carried out will not suffer in the areas of equipment and investment" – it is unfortunately reasonable to expect a significant discrepancy between these strong words and reality in the future.

Ships

After the boom resulting from the reconstruction of the French Navy in the 1950s, French naval building remained on a plateau for a number of years. Then, during the late 1960s, the ambitious *Plan Bleu* set all the Navy dreaming. Awakening to the bitter reality of austere budgeting, the naval staff had to settle for more realistic and, unfortunately, more modest plans.

Many ships then on the drawing board either disappeared or became less sophisticated (as in the case of the AAW version of the C 70 corvette). The French Navy is currently faced with the block obsolescence of many of the fine ships built in the late 1950s and early 1960s. A quick review of the various types currently in service or planned provides a good indication of the likely shape of the French Navy at the end of this century.

Aircraft carriers *Clemenceau* and *Foch* have received a very thorough modernisation, enabling them to carry nuclear-capable aircraft and to soldier on into the late 1990s. However, they were built in the early 1960s and have recently been hard worked as a result of the Lebanon crisis (*Clemenceau* spent 110 days at sea), and their nuclear successors will be more and more urgently needed. The first is already under construction at Brest. Current plans call for one more, but can the French economy foot the bill?

Helicopter carrier *Jeanne d'Arc*, also built in the early 1960s, is long overdue for a modernisation designed to fit her better for her main role of training French Navy cadets and midshipmen. She also has a

reasonable capability as helicopter carrier for ASW or amphibious operations, though this is ultimately limited by her support facilities and lift and hangar dimensions. Her need for an attendant aviso or frigate during training cruises has come in for criticism on cost grounds.

Command cruiser *Colbert* is likely to serve on until the end of the 1990s, having been extensively refitted.

Submarines The ballistic missile submarines form the privileged class of the French Navy, which now has three permanently on patrol. They absorb a large part of the Navy's resources – requiring specialised manpower and the support of minehunters and maritime patrol aircraft – and budget.

Following the arrival of a seventh SNLE of a new type in 1990, *Redoutable* will pay off around 1995. The new class will operate the M4 missile, with improved multiple warheads. The first M4s will be embarked in *Inflexible* as early as 1985, while a second, lighter, version will follow later.

The new nuclear attack submarines, the smallest

Colbert, an 11,300-ton cruiser first commissioned in 1959, is flagship of the Mediterranean Fleet. She was completely reconstructed in 1970–72 and underwent a major refit in 1981–82; this work extended her life until 1995. As with so many large warships today, her gunnery armament of two 100mm and 12 57mm provides only for comparatively close-range engagements, and not for gunfire support of amphibious operations. For longer-range surface engagements she carries four Exocets, and anti-aircraft defence is provided by a twin Masurca launcher.

La Praya (illustrated) and the other three submarines of the *Agosta* class commissioned in 1977–78. This was the last class of non-nuclear submarines to be built for the French Navy, a similar decision having been taken in London some ten years before. Then, at about the time the first French SSN was being laid down at Cherbourg, the Royal Navy began planning to re-introduce non-nuclear submarines. The British problems were twofold: cost and the existence of large areas of shallow water unsuitable for nuclear operations. The French have deep water in the Mediterranean and the outer approaches from the Atlantic, but they may well find new non-nuclears necessary for the shallow waters leading to their main Atlantic ports. (*Giorgio Arra*)

such boats in the world, have been enthusiastically received by the submarine arm. With two already commissioned or under trials, a series of six is scheduled, though the building programme will probably be slowed down. These boats are to be stationed in the Mediterranean, another proof of France's vital interest in this sea.

Duquesne is one of a pair of 6,090-ton ships laid down in 1962–64. She and *Suffren* are considered excellent sea boats and are capable of 34kt. They are larger than the C 70s, carrying two guns, but are otherwise less effective in having no helicopter. Both are soon to undergo a major reconstruction. (*Giorgio Arra*)

Drogou was the third of the 17 ships of the A 69 class of avisos. This 1,170–1,250-ton class is intended for short-range anti-submarine work and overseas operations. *Drogou* is one of the nine fitted with either two or four Exocets. With a speed of 24kt, these small frigates have obvious limitations, though their numbers add to their value as a class. (*Giorgio Arra*)

Cassiopée, the second French Tripartite minehunter, commissioned in 1984. The design results from an agreement between Belgium, France and the Netherlands, with each country building at least ten. Displacing 544 tons each, they can carry out a number of supplementary tasks, for which they embark pre-packed five-ton modules. (*L. & L. van Ginderen*)

Conventional submarines Apart from the four *Agosta*-class boats, this category will diminish in importance as the *Daphne*s are gradually retired. Present studies of conventional submarines are aimed mainly at the export market, in which France has been reasonably successful, having sold submarines to four countries.

Surface forces Latest in a line comprising the 1940 *Volta* class, the 1950 T 47, the *Suffren* class and the superb but not sufficiently numerous *Duguay Trouin* class of the 1970s, the main surface combatant currently produced by the Direction Technique des Constructions Navales (DTCN) is the 3,500-ton C 70 corvette. A well balanced destroyer/frigate, this type will be the main component of the *escadres*, coming in two versions: CODOG for ASW (seven planned) and diesel for AAW (four planned). The very successful ASW version is being fitted with the Flute towed-array sonar, while the AAW design, long delayed, has undergone a number of changes. High-performance diesels supplant the fuel-hungry gas turbines of the ASW version, and systems include modernised Tartar SAMs, recovered from the scrapped T 47 class, a very sophisticated ECM/ESM fit, and advanced fire control. *Suffren* and *Duquesne*, built in the late 1960s, will probably be retired early. The *Duguay Trouin* class is near the end of its useful life.

The 17 A 69 corvettes are maids-of-all-work which perform well, given their limitations. All were built between 1972 and 1984. A high-performance aviso to succeed them is now on the drawing boards, as is the FL 25 replacement for the excellent *avisos escorteurs* and ASW T 47s.

Mine warfare vessels In addition to the Tripartite minehunters (10 planned), it is intended to introduce a new type of minesweeper capable of working at greater depths. All other types will have disappeared or, in the case of the *Circé* class, be near the end of their lives by the year 2000, resulting in a serious reduction in the numbers available.

Patrol vessels Although a new type (PS 400) is being built by Cherbourg Naval Dockyard, numbers will again be far too low in view of the numerous surveillance missions to be carried out in both French and International waters. However, a deep-sea trawler has been converted into the EEZ patrol vessel *Albatros*. She is to be stationed in the French Antarctic territories, a sign that the Falklands lessons have not been ignored.

Amphibious vessels Landing-ship strength will consist mainly of the *Batral* medium transport/landing units (four in service), while the current pair of hard-worked TCDs (Landing Ships Dock) will be succeeded by three TCD 90s, the first of which was to be ordered in 1984. Larger (11,000 tons) and with a much higher speed, they will be built in Brest, bringing some much needed work to the naval dockyard there. Their versatility will be of particular value for overseas interventions or in support of the new *Force d'Action Rapide* (Rapid Reaction Force).

Ouragan, one of the French Navy's pair of Landing Ships (Dock), was commissioned in 1965. Displacing 8,500 tons full load, they can carry three large or ten small helicopters on the main flight deck, plus an additional one or three respectively on a portable platform. Their load of amphibious craft can include two LCTs with 11 light tanks apiece. The first replacement ship was ordered in 1984, with two more to follow at two-year intervals. (*J.Y. Robert*)

Service forces The building effort of the late 1970s has resulted in an adequate number of well designed fleet replenishment vessels (the five-ship *Durance* class, two of which are equipped as command vessels). But the small *Batiments de Soutien Logistique* (Logistic Support Vessels) need replacement, as does the heavy repair ship based in Djibouti.

Equipment

The development of naval systems is a very long process: ten years might easily be devoted to a feasibility study and the development of necessary technology, followed by five more years to prototype production, and another five before first operational deliveries. Production could extend over ten years, with a normal service life of 20–25 years.

The systems planned for the 1990s result from studies begun in the 1970s, will be in full production around 2000, and will still be in service around 2020. Naval staffs and industry are therefore working now to define equipment which will not be introduced until the next century.

The Falklands War's demonstration of the vulnerability of modern vessels prompted the French Navy to rethink several aspects of shipfitting. Emphasis is being placed on damage control; new cabling incorporating fibre-optic techniques; new detection systems embodying optronic technology; the reduction of electromagnetic signatures and noise through the adoption of new shapes, new hull profiles and exhaust-masking materials; and the use of helicopters as full weapon systems both for ASW and anti-surface operations.

Electronic warfare, an early concern of the French

Durance, commissioned in 1976, was the first of four fleet support ships to a new design; the fourth is due in 1986. Displacing 17,800 tons and capable of a range of 9,000 miles at 15kt, *Durance* can carry 7,500 tons of fuel oil, 1,500 tons of diesel fuel, 500 tons of aviation fuel, 130 tons of distilled water, 170 tons of victuals, 150 tons of munitions and 50 tons of naval stores. With four beam transfer positions (two for heavy lifts), one astern position and a helicopter, this class has an enviable combination of capabilities. The second pair (*Var* commissioned in 1983) are designed to carry a Maritime Zone staff, a commando unit of 45 and satellite communications. (*Hartmut Ehlers*)

Navy, is handled by the DAGAIE suite in all major combatants and by SAGAIE in the nuclear carriers and the AAW C 70s.

Air defence against long-range missiles and aircraft will be improved by the increased air superiority resulting from the deployment of advanced aircraft on the new carriers, and by the introduction of the improved Crotale and new Sadral SAMs. The Lebanese experience has resulted in a major effort to devise means of countering all types of air threat, from the Second World War-vintage 500lb bomb to the terrorist suicide attack. This concern also applies to merchant vessels. Gunnery still relies on the standard 100mm weapon for which new ammunition is under development. Systems are being hardened against electromagnetic pulse effects, and modularisation of equipment is being studied with a view to the rapid reconfiguration of the Navy's ever-dwindling number of ships.

Though new platforms such as hydrofoils and airships are being explored with caution, research in other areas is maintained at a high level, as demonstrated by the quality of the naval hardware exported by France. Command, control and communications (C3) is a priority: Syracuse satellite terminals are now installed on major vessels, while the various marks of Senit are fitted aboard all combatants. Airborne early-warning aircraft, an urgent requirement, are still being evaluated, with the Boeing E-3 AWACs apparently in the lead and a French-developed aircraft an unlikely outsider.

Anti-surface warfare The French Navy took a very early interest in the development of anti-ship missiles. The Exocet family gave its major vessels unprecedented firepower. After the earlier MM 38, the later vessels received the lighter and more efficient MM 40, while the AM 39, blooded in the Falklands and Gulf wars, will be carried by the Aéronavale's Super Etendards and Atlantic 2s. The submarine-launched SM 39 will arm the nuclear attack submarines.

A new supersonic anti-ship missile is currently being developed by Aérospatiale jointly with a German partner to take over from Exocet. More difficult to detect and destroy, and more resistant to ECM, it will require beyond-the-horizon midcourse guidance by helicopter, aircraft, submarine or, later, satellite.

Anti-submarine warfare There has been slow progress in submarine detection techniques, the most significant advance being the Flute towed-array sonar, operating at greater depths. Data-processing is greatly improved by the introduction of microprocessors and fibre-optics, which should greatly reduce reaction times and increase the number of targets that can be handled. The integration of all systems (surface, subsurface and air) with a new generation of torpedoes will allow operations at greater depths and higher speeds.

Naval air arm The Aéronavale's Super Etendards will serve aboard the nuclear carriers until their replacement by a new French design, which might be a naval version of the ACX advanced combat aircraft. The new Atlantic Génération 2 is to replace the earlier Atlantic maritime patrol aircraft. Successors for the Lynx and Super Frelon helicopters will have to be developed.

Personnel

In 1983 the French Navy's personnel numbered 69,130 men, comprising 4,230 officers, 27,750 petty officers and 18,850 ratings. The Navy was severely hit by the personnel cuts resulting from the decision to reshape the French armed forces. All categories were affected and, in a period of high unemployment, numbers of highly trained personnel found themselves facing difficulties after leaving the service. The situation was eased somewhat by the demands of the Sawari programme, a huge government export contract signed with Saudi Arabia in 1979. It provides in several stages for four 26,610-ton frigates, two 10,500-ton fleet replenishment vessels, 24 Dauphin helicopters, missiles and other weaponry. The supply of hardware had to be matched by the training of Saudi personnel by highly qualified staff from within the ranks of the French Navy. Chiefly in demand are lieutenant-commanders, lieutenants and senior petty officers, especially in the technical trades. The high level of sophistication of the vessels, much envied by the French Navy itself, calls for very competent personnel. In general the programme is causing strains within the posting system, though it does have the positive effect of creating a comfortable transition to civilian life.

A highly technical force, the Navy relies mainly on men joining for longer than the current 12 months of national service, although a high proportion of ratings are conscripts. Given the amount of training possible in 12 months and the good initial level of education, it is possible to make adequate use of the conscripts, especially when they show some enthusiasm. The *Préparation Militaire Marine* (elementary naval training) scheme has in recent years publicised the Navy among the young and given them a degree of basic training before their national service.

If a man wants to volunteer for long service, the Navy now has more choice and can be demanding as to education and standards. After the difficult years of the 1970s, the growing unemployment rate and worsening economic situation have resulted in a steady flow of young men trying to join the Navy, while the rush to get into civilian jobs on completion of training has tailed off. At the same time, rates of pay are now comparable with civilian levels, and job security is better.

While the situation on the lower decks is therefore satisfactory, recent reorganisation has resulted in petty officers generally being much younger than before. Consequently they often lack the weight of knowledge and wisdom of their predecessors, which is disturbing in view of their essential role in the naval organisation. This is offset by a high general level of training (one third of all naval personnel are under training at any one time), and an increased ratio of petty officers to ratings.

As part of the Government's campaign to alleviate the social tensions generated by the economic crisis, the armed services are seeking to improve the quality of national service and are now offering 4–24 months of extra service to conscripts who wish to acquire more

France has 16 ships and yachts employed on training duties. The eight ships of the *Léopard* class were all commissioned in 1982–83. *Lynx*, one of the second pair built, displaces 463 tons, has a speed of 15kt and is capable of carrying 21 trainees. This class shows the importance the French Navy attaches to its training programmes. (*L. & L. van Ginderen*)

training. These measures, though politically motivated, will make their mark on the Navy.

Another new development is the creation of wider opportunities for women in the Navy. They now have access to all non-combat jobs, and for an experimental five-year period they will be able to enter certain technical schools and go to sea on logistic or support vessels. Architect of the scheme is General Valérie André, the first woman general in the French forces, and there can be no question that she has a difficult job on her hands. Women in the Navy are seen as intruders in a man's world, and as extra competition for the jobs and plum postings in a diminishing Navy. Then there is the resentment of wives ashore and the practical difficulties encountered in ships not designed for female crew. General André has five years in which to overcome a great deal of prejudice: if she fails her scheme will be dismissed as just another political gimmick in a pre-election period.

The officers of the French Navy generally all have the same social and educational background. Some family names appear regularly in the Navy List, but in a shrinking fleet the chances of promotion to Flag rank are diminishing. Although all are required to achieve an increasingly high standard of professionalism, there is a tendency amongst some of the technical officers to lose their enthusiasm for the Navy and to look upon it as just another job. In other branches a fall-off in interest may result from the recent cuts in flying hours to the very minimum for proficiency, and from the disappearance of so many of the "little bridges," the small patrol craft, minesweepers and miscellaneous vessels which give young officers their first, invaluable experience of command.

Conclusion

The French Navy of the year 2000 will be smaller, more compact and manned by a highly professional force. One can only hope that the cuts now in progress and prospect will not affect it too severely. Its missions will be very diverse, with commitments including the defence of French coastal waters, trade and shipping; the surveillance, with inadequate means, of an enormous Exclusive Economic Zone; the protection of French territories and interests overseas; and participation in the defence of western Europe. Financial restrictions will demand greater adaptability and flexibility, to be achieved by a major reorganisation. Though numbers will be smaller, individual quality will be higher. There is however an irreducible minimum, and it is to be hoped that French naval strength will not fall below it in the next 15 years. The *Force d'Action Rapide* will no doubt be very useful, but there will still be a need, for instance, for a patrol vessel to loiter in the Bay of Biscay.

Another big uncertainty concerns the present French overseas territories and departments: are the disturbances of the past few months in New Caledonia and the French Antilles (West Indies) isolated phenomena or the beginning of more serious and violent movements towards independence? If the latter, France is going to need a credible oceanic navy to protect its interests. But such a force cannot be created overnight, and it is vital that French politicians understand this and resist any temptation to run down a highly professional force. The modest levels of current deliveries, the orders designed only to get minor programmes back on schedule, delays in the new construction programmes, reductions in spending on fuel and the dockyards: these expedients can only mean a loss of capability in the long run.

The French shipbuilding and naval equipment industries are well known for their quality, but export orders (harder and harder to win in the face of bitter competition from abroad) will not be enough to keep the industries dynamic and capable of responding quickly in an emergency.

Past crises have always taught their lessons. Lebanon taught the French Navy how to support a force 1,600 miles from its main base, how to co-operate more closely with its merchant fleet, how to improve its air defences while working in a narrow sea space. This adaptability and readiness to learn are naval qualities. *Faire avec* ("to make do with") is almost a motto. But these attributes must be matched by a political will to maintain the material quality of the Navy, and the prospects are not encouraging.

Throughout its long history the French Navy has been through periods of splendour and of utter misery. After its almost complete destruction during the Second World War it was resurrected to become the third strongest navy in the world. Let us hope that the low period we are going through represents nothing more than a transition towards a streamlined, highly professional and powerful navy with which to enter the 21st century.

US Navy under way again

Samuel L. Morison

The eminent naval historian Samuel Eliot Morison once said: "If the deadly missiles with their apocalyptic warheads are ever launched at America the Navy will still be out on the blue water fighting for her, and the nation or alliance that survives will be the one that retains command of the oceans." Four years ago, as a result of the Carter Administration's policy of a "defence second to none," there was a lot of doubt that the US Navy could even get out to the blue water, let alone fight. By the last year of the Carter Administration America's capability to fight a war had sunk so low that to some it appeared non-existent. This lack of capability was made painfully clear by the Iranian hostage crisis and the resulting aborted rescue attempt.

The problem revealed itself in a number of ways within the US Navy. Because there was not enough money to arm fully all of the Navy's front-line units, ships returning from deployment would have to cross-

deck munitions to top up the magazines of the vessels relieving them on station. Overhauls were postponed from year to year, causing the material condition of ships to deteriorate. Construction programmes needed to avoid imminent block obsolescence were continually put off. Ships had to be decommissioned without

FFG-13, seventh of the *Oliver Hazard Perry* class of 3,585-ton (full load) frigates, was named after the distinguished naval historian Samuel Eliot Morison, grandfather of the author of this article. With two LAMPS helicopters and Standard missiles, anti-submarine torpedo tubes, a 76mm gun and Phalanx, the 51 ships of this class have an all-round, if limited, capability. Propelled by two gas turbines and one shaft, they are capable of 29kt. All have a hull-mounted sonar, and later ships also carry a tactical towed-array system (SQR-19). (*US Navy*)

replacement, thereby diminishing the Navy's resources while its commitments remained the same. At the height of the Vietnam War the US Navy had 974 deployable ships. By February 1, 1981, this was down to only 479.

When President Reagan first took office, he, Defence Secretary Caspar Weinberger and Navy Secretary John H. Lehman revived the early-1970s goal of a modern, 600-ship Navy to meet the challenge of the ever-expanding Soviet Navy. If current trends continue, this should be achieved in Fiscal Year (FY) 1989. The required increase in strength was to have been attained by doubling the number of ships under construction and making a prompt start on long-overdue replacement and expansion programmes, especially in the areas of anti-air warfare, mine warfare and amphibious warfare. At the beginning of President Reagan's second term, how many of these objectives have been achieved, and what can the Navy expect from another four years of Reagan-style government?

Submarines

The US Navy's submarine force comprises strategic missile submarines (SSBNs), the seagoing element of the deterrent triad, and nuclear-powered attack submarines (SSNs), designed to seek out and destroy enemy boats.

In January 1981 the SSBN force consisted of 31 *Lafayette/Benjamin Franklin*-class boats armed with Poseidon C-3 missiles and seven old *George Washington/Ethan Allen*-class boats armed with the obsolete Polaris A-3. The latter two classes were then in the process of being phased out of the strategic force. The first of the new *Ohio*-class SSBNs, capable of carrying 24 Trident I C-4 missiles, was under construc-tion, but some two years behind schedule. *Ohio* (SSBN-726) finally commissioned on November 11, 1981. At the same time, 12 of the *Lafayette/Benjamin Franklin* class were being converted to handle the Trident I missile. This work was carried out between September 24, 1978, and December 10, 1982. Current plans call for the construction of 24 *Ohio*-class submarines at a rate of one authorised per year until FY 1997. The 24th boat would therefore commission in about 2003. By that time the SSBN force would consist entirely of *Ohio*-class boats carrying a total of 576 Trident I/II missiles with ten warheads per missile. The *Lafayette/Benjamin Franklin* class is due to be retired by the late 1990s.

The 600-ship Navy is intended to include a force of 100 multi-mission modern SSNs by the mid-1990s. For this a sharp acceleration in construction has been necessary. The final Carter Administration defence budget (FY 1981) requested a single SSN for construction, while a supplement sent to Congress shortly after the Reagan Administration took power requested a second. By Fy 1984 the number requested per budget had risen to four, a level which will be maintained up to and including FY 1989.

The SSBN and SSN forces are also being improved qualitatively. SSBN improvements centre on the development of the Trident II missile and the Mk 500

George Bancroft, one of the *Lafayette* class of ballistic missile submarines, commissioned in January 1966. The 31 boats of this and the similar *Benjamin Franklin* classes each carry 16 launch tubes designed originally for Polaris missiles. Between September 1978 and December 1982 12 of these submarines, including *George Bancroft*, were converted to launch Trident 1 missiles. (*Giorgio Arra*)

manoeuvring re-entry vehicle (MARV), designed to evade anti-ballistic missile (ABM) defences. Trident II, with its 6,000-mile range, will permit the SSBNs to patrol further afield, further reducing their chances of being located by Soviet anti-submarine sensors. Scheduled to become operational in FY 1989, the missile will be initially fitted in new-construction SSBNs, beginning with the ninth *Ohio*-class hull (SSBN-734). The first eight hulls (SSBN-726/733) will be retrofitted with the missile during their first post-FY 1989 over-

hauls. The Mk 500 MARV, a replacement for the existing multiple independently targeted (MIRV) warheads, is compatible with both the Trident I and II missiles. The MARV warheads will be able to evade anti-ballistic missile (ABM) interceptors.

The most important SSN improvement is a completely new design of submarine, projected to replace the *Sturgeon* class. The prototype, expected to cost $1.6 billion, is scheduled for the FY 1989 budget, with series production beginning under FY 1991 at a unit

▲ *Patrick Henry* belongs to the world's first class of nuclear-powered ballistic missile submarines, the 16-Polaris *George Washington* class. The forerunners of a force which eventually totalled 41 boats, they were operational from 1960 to October 1981. As the *Ohio* class began to commission, the senior class in the US SSBN force began to be paid off or converted to other tasks. *Patrick Henry* and two others currently operate as SSNs in training and secondary roles. (*Giorgio Arra*)

▼*La Jolla* (SSN-701) is the 14th of the *Los Angeles* class of attack submarines. Of 6,900 tons dived displacement and with a diving depth of 1,475ft, they have their armament of four torpedo tubes amidships and carry Mk 48 torpedoes, Subroc and Tomahawk. From SSN-688 (first of class) to SSN-720 the Tomahawk load will be tube-launched; from SSN-721 onwards the missiles will be carried in vertical launch tubes fitted in the bow between the inner and outer hulls. This class continues the USN practice of having a single screw, the primary power source being a pressurised-water reactor. (*Giorgio Arra*)

Drum is one of the *Sturgeon* class of SSNs, which commissioned between 1967 and 1975. Of 4,640 tons dived displacement and fitted with four midships tubes, these submarines have the same propulsion system as the *Thresher* class but are slightly larger and probably marginally slower, though still capable of over 30kt dived.

ing facilities and of the systems needed for operations under the icecaps. Finally, the Submarine Advanced Combat System (SUBACS) is scheduled to be installed in all SSNs, beginning with those authorised in the FY 1983 programme.

cost of $1.0 billion. All *Sturgeon/Los Angeles*-class SSNs are to be armed with encapsulated Harpoon anti-ship missiles and Tomahawk cruise missiles. All of the *Sturgeon* class and the first 33 units of the *Los Angeles* class will carry their Harpoons and Tomahawks as part of the torpedo load and will launch them through the torpedo tubes. From the 34th, *Chicago* (SSN-721), the *Los Angeles* boats will have a 15-tube vertical launch system (VLS) mounted in the bow, between the inner and outer hulls. This will enable them to carry Tomahawks without detriment to their torpedo capacity. *Boston* (SSN-703), *Baltimore* (SSN-704), *Atlanta* (SSN-712) and *Houston* (SSN-713) are the first SSNs to be fitted to carry Tomahawk. Other improvements to the *Los Angeles* class include the installation of minelay-

Aircraft carriers

Though the United States Navy has long been supreme in the area of fixed-wing aircraft operations, American carrier aviation reached a comparative low point during the Carter Administration. Inheriting only 12 deployable carriers, a 13th ship always undergoing a Service Life Extension Programme (SLEP) overhaul, and one contingency ship (*Coral Sea*, CV-43) with no air wing, President Reagan established a goal of 15 deployable carrier battle groups by the beginning of the next decade. The first step towards this was the return of *Coral Sea* to fully deployable status. Then came the establishment of a 13th carrier air wing under the FY 1983 programme. The FY 1984 programme

Carl Vinson is the third nuclear-propelled aircraft carrier of the *Nimitz* class. Her full-load tonnage is 91,487, her two reactors provide steam for four geared turbines with a total output of 260,000shp, and she is capable of more than 30kt. Her aircraft complement is 90-plus, she has four steam catapults and a ship's company (including air wing) of 6,300, and she cost in excess of $2 billion. (*Gilbert Gyssels*)

approve construction of two *Nimitz*-class carriers in one budget. Considering the sanguinary battles that have raged between Congress and various other administrations over carrier construction, this was indeed a coup. The Administration supported the request by claiming that it would seek the second carrier in FY 1985 anyway, and that valuable savings

established a 14th carrier air wing, while the FY 1986 programme calls for the 15th wing, to be manned by reservists. If approved, the 15th wing would be therefore contribute to the modernisation of Naval Reserve aviation.

Most important of all, however, was a remarkable feat by President Reagan, who persuaded Congress to

Enterprise was the largest warship ever built when she was completed in 1961. Her full-load displacement is now 90,970 tons. She has eight reactors and four turbines yielding a total of 280,000shp. She carries about 90 aircraft and has a ship's company (including air wing) of 5,500. Her final cost was $451.3 million, a sum which so startled the authorities that plans for a further five were cancelled. (*Giorgio Arra*)

Kitty Hawk, the first of four carriers to an improved *Forrestal* design, joined the fleet in April 1961, seven months before *Enterprise* commissioned. Eight Foster-Wheeler boilers feed four turbines yielding 280,000shp and a maximum speed of over 30kt. Ship's company totals 4,950 and building cost was $265.2 million, about 55% that of *Enterprise*. (*Giorgio Arra*)

would result from approving the two ships at the same time. The two new carriers became *Abraham Lincoln* (CVN-72) and *George Washington* (CVN-73). With *Theodore Roosevelt* (CVN-71), approved in FY 1980 after two years of furious resistance from the Carter Administration, this makes three carriers now under construction. When CVN-71 commissions in January 1986 she will become the Navy's 14th deployable carrier. CVN-72, due to commission in January 1990, will be the 15th, while CVN-73, due to commission in 1991, will replace *Coral Sea*, which will in turn relieve the by then nearly 50-year-old *Lexington* (AVT-16) as training carrier. While the active total will by this time be 16 ships (CV-41, 59-64, 66 and 67, CVN-65 and 68-73), one will always be undergoing SLEP overhaul. It is planned to keep *Midway* (CV-41) deployable to the turn of the century.

The cost of a modern carrier has risen from the $188.9 million for *Forrestal* (CV-59) to an average of $3.3 billion each for CVN-72 and 73. On October 1, 1985, *Forrestal*, the first of the post-war carriers, will be 30 years old, once considered to be the limit of such a ship's effective life. The rest of the carrier fleet – with the exception of *John F. Kennedy*, commissioned in 1968, and the *Nimitz* class – will reach this point at almost yearly intervals thereafter. Time and money are too short to permit the replacement of these ships.

Indeed, such a programme would be physically impossible, American carrier construction being limited to one shipyard, Newport News Shipbuilding and Drydock Co. So was born the Service Life Extension Programme (SLEP), which at an average unit cost of between $700 and $775 million over 28 months adds 10–15 years to each ship's active life. Work performed includes the up-dating of all electronics, replacement of catapults and electrical cabling, boiler retubing, and the fitting of NATO Sea Sparrow launchers. *Saratoga* (CV-60) has completed her SLEP, *Forrestal* is in the dockyard, and *Independence* (CV-62), *Kitty Hawk* (CV-63) and *Constellation* (CV-64) will follow in that order. The SLEP of *Ranger* (CV-61) has been indefinitely deferred.

Surface combatants

The three major surface combatant programmes now under way will provide both the escorts needed for the extra carrier battle groups and replacements for the existing force. These ships are the *Ticonderoga*-class (Aegis) guided missile cruisers (CG), the *Arleigh Burke*-class (Aegis) guided missile destroyers (DDG), and the *Oliver Hazard Perry*-class guided missile frigates (FFG). Related to this effort is the *Iowa*-class battleship (BB) reactivation project.

It is currently planned to build 26 *Ticonderoga*s, though this is likely to be raised to 30 in the FY 1986 programme. Two ships are in commission, 11 are under construction or on order, and the remaining 13 are scheduled for FY 1985–1989. These ships are designed to be the air-defence lynchpins of the carrier battle groups. The very advanced Aegis system is

Except for the Japanese *Yamato* class, the four ships of the *Iowa* class were the largest battleships ever built. After action in the last two years of the Second World War, five years in mothballs were followed by action off Korea for *New Jersey* and her three sisters. From April 1968 to the end of 1969 *New Jersey* operated off Vietnam before once more returning to Bremerton and mothballs. After a series of differences, Congress agreed to *New Jersey*'s reactivation and return to the fleet. She was taken in hand on October 1, 1981, and recommissioned on December 28, 1982. From then on she was kept busy: she was despatched to the Far East, recalled before she had completed her cruise and sent to Central America, and then transferred at speed to the Eastern Mediterranean. This photograph shows the new electronics fit, three of her four Phalanx CIWS, and three of her six 5in turrets. (*Giorgio Arra*)

Texas is one of the four *Virginia*-class nuclear-propelled guided missile cruisers. She has a full-load displacement of 10,000 tons and carries an armament of eight Harpoons, two twin Mk 26 launchers for Standard and Asroc missiles, and two 5in guns. The almost unbelievable omission of a helicopter from the preceding *California* class was rectified in the *Virginia*s, which carry two helicopters in a hangar beneath the fantail landing deck. (*Giorgio Arra*)

capable of detecting and intercepting high-speed aircraft and cruise missiles, and in a major test in early 1984 *Ticonderoga* (CG-47) shot down 11 out of 12 drones simulating attacking aircraft and cruise missiles; the 12th drone crashed into the sea before reaching the target area.

Major improvements to this class begin with CG-52, in which two 122-missile vertical launch systems (VLS) will replace the two twin Mk 26 launchers. The AN/SPY-1B improved Aegis will be installed in CG-58 onwards.

While the class has been attacked by the General Accounting Office (GAO), the investigative arm of Congress, as too costly and too unstable, these criticisms seem to have little foundation. The very high capability of Aegis actually makes these ships extremely cost-effective. As to "instability," the GAO investigators never even visited *Ticonderoga*, let alone watched her perform at sea.

Arleigh Burke, carrying the smaller SPY-1D version of Aegis, is essentially a less expensive *Ticonderoga*. The *Burke*s are due to replace the *Leahy* and *Belknap*-class CGs and the *Coontz*-class DDGs. Besides escorting the Navy's carrier battle and surface action groups, they will also be the primary protection of amphibious task forces and groups of underway replenishment/support ships. Each will be armed with one 90-missile VLS, two Vulcan/Phalanx close-in weapons systems (CIWS), a mix of Standard (SAM), Tomahawk (cruise) and Harpoon (SSM) missiles, and one lightweight 5in/54 gun mount. At an average of $900 million to $1.1 billion each, these ships have been criticised on cost grounds, as well as for their lack of helicopter storage and maintenance facilities. Each is fitted with a helicopter landing deck and rearming and refuelling facilities, but no hangar. A Sea Hawk (LAMPS III) helicopter will be detached as necessary from another ship in the task force, so the reasoning goes. But what if all the helicopters in the task force are otherwise engaged?

The sense behind this criticism was acknowledged, and the proposed force cut from 60 to 29 ships. It is now planned to build an improved version, beginning with the FY 1993 programme, incorporating a helicopter hangar and complete facilities for the support of a Sea Hawk.

The third surface combatant construction programme is now coming to a close. Of the 50 *Oliver Hazard Perry*-class (FFG-7) guided missile frigates authorised, 38 are now in commission and 12 at various stages of construction. They were designed to serve as escorts in low-threat areas, hence their emphasis on anti-ship, anti-missile and anti-aircraft defence, as compared with the anti-submarine bias of previous frigate classes. Early units of the class – FFG-7, FFG-9/16 and FFG-19/27 – are being transferred to the Naval Reserve Force (NRF), along with six *Knox*-class frigates (FF), in an effort to improve the capabilities of this long neglected formation. *Duncan* (FFG-10) was transferred on January 21, 1984, followed by *Oliver Hazard Perry* (FFG-7) on May 31 and *Clifton Sprague* (FFG-16) on August 31. Also contributing to the decision to transfer the *Perry*s is the fact that they cannot handle the LAMPS III anti-submarine helicopter, being restricted to the older LAMPS I. The transfers are due to continue until January 1988.

The *Iowa*-class battleships had accumulated an average of less than 12 years of service life each, on hulls designed to last for 30, when it was decided to reacti-

Ticonderoga is the first of the CG-47 class, gas-turbine ships displacing 9,600 tons full load and carrying the Aegis weapon control system. Visible here on the massive superstructure are two of the four fixed faces of the SPY-1A radar. Aegis can cope with several hundred targets simultaneously and control a dozen or more missiles in the air at one time through the four Mk 99 fire-control systems. The hull design is basically the same as that of the *Spruance*-class destroyers, but the armament includes two Mk 26 launchers for Standard SM-2MR missiles or Asroc in place of the NATO Sea Sparrow and separate Asroc launcher in the *Spruance*s. (*Michael D. J. Lennon*)

Belknap was the first of a class of nine ships which were originally designated DLGs but reclassified as cruisers in 1975. She was severely damaged in a collision with the carrier *John F. Kennedy* in 1975. Four and a half years later she rejoined the fleet with a number of modifications and improvements. Comparison with *Ticonderoga* shows the changes that have been made to this type of ship over the last 20 years. (*Giorgio Arra*)

vate them. The first reactivation was approved in FY 1982 after stiff opposition from some quarters in Congress. The scales were tipped in favour of the programme by the fact that these ships offer a quick and significant increase in capability at about one third the cost and time needed to construct a *Virginia*-class nuclear-powered guided missile cruiser (CGN). Fitted with Tomahawk cruise missiles, Harpoon surface-to-surface missiles, improved electronics and communications, and, of course, those awesome 16in turrets, they

It was a fitting tribute to a great admiral when the first of the USN's new ASW destroyers was named *Spruance* in 1973. She was the name ship of a class of 31, the last being commissioned in March 1983. In June 1978 the first of four *Spruance*-class variants was laid down for the Imperial Iranian Navy, a 1974 order for six having been cut by a third. In 1979, following the departure of the Shah, the whole order was cancelled. *Callaghan* (illustrated) was the second ship of the Iranian order, which was taken over in its entirety by the USN later in 1979. The main difference from the *Spruance* class lies in the use, as in *Ticonderoga*, of two twin Mk 26 launchers for Standard and Asroc missiles in place of separate Sea Sparrow and Asroc launchers. (*Giorgio Arra*)

soon is the Rolling Airframe Missile (RAM), which has just successfully completed development and should enter production in FY 1985. All these improvements will keep the surface combatant force effective until the end of the century, by which time the *Ticonderoga*-class CGs and *Arleigh Burke*-class DDGs will have been produced in sufficient quantities to replace existing ships.

Mine warfare

The Soviet Navy maintains the world's largest mine warfare force and mine inventory, over 280,000 in total. In the face of this threat, the US Navy's mine-sweeping capability consists of 21 30-year-old ocean minesweepers (MSO) and 23 RH-53 Sea Stallion helicopters. For the first time since before the Second World War the Navy has begun a mine warfare moder-nisation programme without being forced into it by a conflict. Two new classes – the *Avenger* mine counter-measures ships (MCM) and the *Cardinal* minehunters (MSH) are being built to replace the MSOs.

The *Avengers* are designed to serve as combination minehunter/minesweepers, with special emphasis on sweeping or neutralising the latest types of Soviet mine. In addition to acoustic, mechanical and moored sweep-ing gear, they will be fitted with the new Mine Neutral-isation System (MNS). The originally planned total of 21 units of this class was cut back to 14 under the FY 1984 programme. Costing an average of $87.1 million each, they will be constructed of oak and fir with glass-reinforced plastic (GRP) sheathing. The first eight ships will spend a year working up with the active fleet before transferring to the Naval Reserve Force. The remainder of the class will stay with the active fleet. Each ship will be equipped with the new but already obsolete AN/SQQ-30 minehunting sonar, which is

will be able to act as the core of surface action groups, perform flag-showing missions, and provide gunfire support in amphibious operations. *New Jersey* (BB-62) was recommissioned on December 28, 1982, followed by *Iowa*, approved in the FY 1983 programme, on April 18, 1984. The third reactivation, *Missouri* (BB-63), was originally programmed for the FY 1985 budget. It was then brought forward to FY 1984 and is now under way at Long Beach Naval Shipyard, with recommissioning scheduled for July 1986. The last reactivation, *Wisconsin* (BB-64), is scheduled for FY 1987. Costs range from $329.0 million for *New Jersey*, the most modern of the four ships, to an estimated $458.4 million for *Wisconsin*.

The rest of the Navy's surface combatant force is the subject of a continuing effort to extend service lives and upgrade capabilities. This includes re-equipping all missile-armed ships with the new Standard (SM-2) surface to air missile, a marked improvement over the SM-1 version, improving shipboard radars and weapon control systems, and fitting Vulcan/Phalanx CIWS mounts, the new AN/SLQ-32(V) electronic counter-measures system, and the Mk 23 target-acquisition radar for NATO Sea Sparrow. Due to reach the fleet

only a minor improvement on the AN/SQQ-14 install-ed in the MSOs. The next real improvement in US minehunting sonar will come in FY 1989, when the first AN/SQQ-32 is due to enter service. This system, developed jointly by the Navy and Thomson-CSF, is a marked improvement on SQQ-14 and SSQ-30. AN/SQQ-32 will be fitted in all *Avenger*-class ships, begin-ning in 1990.

The *Cardinal* class is designed to supplement the *Avenger*s, but unlike the latter will not be capable of deploying without the assistance of a mother ship. First of class, *Cardinal* (MSH-1), was authorised in the FY 1984 programme at a cost of $65.0 million. Design of these ships is the subject of a competition between Marinette Marine, offering a conventional hull, and Bell Aerospace, with an air-cushion vehicle. Each will spend a year working up with the fleet before transfer-ring to the Naval Reserve Force.

Other mine warfare developments include the acquisition of the MH-53D Sea Stallion advanced minesweeping helicopter, and the Mine Warfare Har-bour Defence Project, otherwise known as COOP. A total of 44 MH-53Ds is planned, with funds for initial production being requested in the FY 1985 pro-gramme. These aircraft will replace the existing force of 21 RH-53s, resulting in a more than 100% increase in numbers and a 200% improvement in capability. The COOP programme is based on 10 former training craft from the US Naval Academy and 12 trawlers confiscated from drug smugglers. All will be converted into auxiliary minesweepers and classified as mine-sweeping survey boats (MSSB). Though their primary mission will be to survey harbour entrances in prepara-tion for minesweeping operations, they will also be able to tackle mines themselves, mainly by means of fishing nets. The 22 MSSBs will be stationed in various ports throughout the country and manned by reservists. MSSB-1 is currently stationed at Charleston, South Carolina, and MSSB-2, now under conversion at Charleston, will be stationed at Galveston, Texas. Both are converted trawlers.

While these programmes will go a long way towards upgrading the US Navy's mine warfare capabilities, they are by no means enough. The Navy plans to keep the ports clear of mines "by priority". Does that mean that merchant ships would have to wait outside ports with less priority, laying themselves open to submarine attack? There is also the question of minesweeper los-ses: during the Korean War no fewer than four US and South Korean minesweepers struck mines and sank during the clearing of Wonsan Harbour. The minimum practicable force is about 30 of each of the *Cardinal* and *Avenger* classes, though ideally the Navy would have double this figure.

Amphibious warfare

The expansion and modernisation of the US Navy's amphibious assault force was one of the major defence initiatives of President Reagan's first term. It centres on three major construction programmes and SLEP-style overhauls for the *Austin*-class amphibious trans-port docks (LPD). The goal is a lift capability of one Marine Amphibious Force (MAF), comprising 45,600 troops, 6,300 Navy personnel and an air wing with supporting elements, and one Marine Amphibious Brigade (MAB) of 16,500 troops by 1994. Also included in the plan is a switch to a new method of amphibious assault under which the high-speed air-cushion landing craft now being built would be launched from over the horizon, where the parent ship would be safer.

Belleau Wood, commissioned in 1978, is one of the five-ship *Tarawa* class of amphibious assault ships, which under pre-sent plans will be joined by ships of the slightly larger *Wasp* class from 1990. Displacing 39,300 tons full load, the *Tarawa*s can carry 1,703 troops as against a ship's company of 902. To provide landing facilities six LCM6, 19 Sea Stallion or 26 Sea Knight helicopters can be carried. Harrier V/STOL aircraft can also be embarked in place of helicopters. (*Giorgio Arra*)

Much smaller than the *Tarawa* class, the seven-strong *Iwo Jima* class, of which *New Orleans* (illustrated) is the sixth, were commissioned in 1961–70. Their helicopter complement is proportionately smaller than that of the *Tarawas*. As they ultimately pay off they will be relieved by the *Wasp* class. (*US Navy*)

The US Navy plans to acquire 108 Landing Craft Air Cushion (LCAC). These craft will allow the US Marine Corps to carry out amphibious landings with little fear of mining and beach obstacles. LCAC-1 was rolled out on May 2, 1984. (*Bell-Halter*)

Most important of the new ships under construction are the *Wasp*-class multi-purpose amphibious assault ships (LHD). Slightly bigger than the *Tarawa*-class general-purpose amphibious assault ships (LHA), which they closely resemble in design, they will be used to transport troops, vehicles and cargo. Each will be able to carry three of the new air-cushion landing craft – (LCAC) in its well deck. Cargo area will be 100,900ft², with an additional 22,000ft² for vehicles. Normal aircraft complement will be 30 helicopters of various sizes and 6–8 AV-8B Harrier II V/STOL aircraft. These ships can also be converted easily into V/STOL aircraft carriers for use in the sea control, tactical air support or anti-submarine warfare roles. Aircraft complement for these purposes would comprise 20 AV-8Bs and up to six Sea Hawk ASW helicopters.

It was initially planned to build the *Wasps* replace one for one the seven *Iwo Jima*-class amphibious assault ships (LPH), which are due to retire in the late 1990s, but the projected force level has since been raised to 11 ships. First of class was authorised in the FY 1984 programme, with the remaining ten units to be requested at the rate of one per year in FY 1986–95. The main difference between the new class and the *Tarawas* is a superstructure two decks lower, the command, control and communications spaces having been moved to within the hull to reduce the likelihood of a "cheap kill".

The second big construction programme concerns the *Whidbey Island*-class dock landing ships (LSD).

Originally six of the class were to have been built to replace the eight 20-year-old *Thomaston*-class LSDs. The Carter Administration wanted to cancel the entire programme but yielded to heavy Congressional pressure for retention of the prototype. Then the first Reagan five-year programme (FY 1982–85) reinstated the original six ships and added another four. February 1982 saw an increase in projected force level to 12, only for the FY 1985 budget to revise it to ten standard ships plus four Modified *Whidbey Island*s (LSD-51/54). Originally designated LPDX or LDD-17, the new class will look almost identical with the first ten ships from the outside but will have a smaller well deck accommodating two LCACs instead of four. The resulting extra space will be used to carry more vehicles and cargo, providing a better match with Marine Corps lift requirements.

Most novel of the three construction programmes is

the Landing Craft, Air-Cushion (LCAC), designed to operate from LHA, LPD, LSD and LHD-type ships and based primarily on the JEFF (B) prototype. The 1,800ft² well deck of each craft will be able to carry up to 60 tons of cargo. Projected force level is 90 craft, down from 108. The first 12 have been requested in the FY 1984 programme, nine are covered by the FY 1985 budget, and full production at a rate of 12 a year is scheduled to start in FY 1986. LCACs will have replaced all the Navy's LCM (8)s by FY 1995 and will start supplanting the LCUs in FY 1996. The first, LCAC-1, was delivered on May 2, 1984. The one weakness of the design is the fact that the cargo deck is uncovered, leaving troops and cargo exposed to weather and sea spray. The Soviet Navy operates over 70 amphibious air-cushion vehicles of five different classes, and every one of them has a covered well deck. Bell-Halter of New Orleans is LCAC prime contractor.

Each Austin-class SLEP will take about 14 months and add 10–15 years to service life. The first is scheduled for the FY 1987 programme, followed by two in FY 1988, three in FY 1989, four in FY 1990 and the last in FY 1992.

Auxiliary ships

Construction of auxiliary ships peaked during the 1970s and activity in this area is now largely confined to the modernisation of underway replenishment forces. During the 1970s the Samuel Gompers and Yellowstone-class destroyer tenders (AD) replaced the Second World War-built Cascade, Klondike and Dixie-class ADs, while the new L.Y. Spear and Emory S. Land-class submarine tenders (AS) replaced most of the Fulton-class AS. The new Cimarron class (AO-177/180, 186) replaced the last of the old Cimarron-class (AO-22) AOs. Other replacement programmes included the construction of a cable repair

San Bernardino was the 11th of the 20 Newport-class LSTs, commissioned in 1969–72. With a higher speed (20kt) than previous LSTs, they were able to maintain station in a mixed amphibious force. They are the first USN LSTs to depart from the original British bow door design, which would have made the required maximum speed unattainable. Vehicle stowage capacity is 500 tons, and landings are effected over a 112ft ramp in the bows. (US Navy)

ship (ARC), Zeus (ARC-7), and a large dry dock (ARDM).

Current construction centres on the 18 Henry J. Kaiser-class oilers (AO), the Stalwart-class ocean surveillance ships (AGOS) and the Safeguard-class salvage ships (ARS). The Henry J. Kaiser AO is a modified and enlarged version of the new Cimarron design. Four of the planned 18 ships have been authorised in the FY 1984 programme; the next 12 will be requested at a rate of three per year until FY 1988, and the final pair in FY 1989. The class will have a cargo capacity of 180,000 barrels and will replace the two surviving "jumboised" old Cimarron-class units (AO-98 and 99) and all the Mispillion and Neosho-class AOs.

The Stalwart-class AGOS are designed to carry and deploy the new Surtass sonar and transmit the resulting information to shore bases for evaluation. The Stalwarts will supplement fixed surveillance systems by extending coverage to areas not monitored at present, and will provide a back-up if any of the fixed systems become inoperative. Twelve of the class were authorised in the FY 1979–81 programmes at an average cost of $35.0 million each. The first two of the class have entered service, four are under construction and the remainder are on order. A further six, added to the programme by the Reagan Administration, will be requested in FY 1985 and 1986 at a unit cost of $64.0 million.

At present the US Navy's entire salvage ship (ARS)

Puget Sound is one of six modern destroyer tenders which are very similar in design to the new USN submarine tenders. Displacing 20,500 tons full load, she can support six destroyers at one time and also has nuclear powerplant support facilities. *Puget Sound* became 6th Fleet flagship in the Mediterranean in July 1980. (*Giorgio Arra*)

---

force consists of Second World War-built vessels. The four-unit *Safeguard* class will replace all ships and complement the *Edenton*-class salvage and rescue ships (ATS). The first of class, *Safeguard* (ARS-50), is scheduled to commission in February 1985 and the last, *Grapple* (ARS-53), in November 1985.

An interesting reactivation in this area is that of *Sphinx*, the Navy's last small repair ship (ARL). She is scheduled to recommission in April 1985 for use on general repair tasks and as tender to the *Pegasus*-class PHMs. Though *Sphinx* is nearly 40 years old, her service life is less than half that. She was completely modernised during her reactivation for her last commission, Vietnam 1968–70. Her return to service allows the *Pegasus* class to deploy overseas, something they could not do without a mother ship.

Finally, two new survey ships (AGS) are to replace the two surviving *Dutton*-class AGS. The Navy originally intended to convert two commercial cargo ships for this task, but Congress vetoed this plan on the grounds that the conversions would have too short a service life to be cost-effective. Average cost of the ships will be $122.5 million; both are in the FY 1985 programme.

Future programmes include the "jumboising" of the new *Cimarron*-class AOs. This class has been severely criticised, and its numbers cut back to five from the

---

Merrimack is one of the five *Cimarron*-class oilers, which commissioned in 1981–83. They are capable of 20kt and carry 120,000 barrels of fuel, enough for two complete refuellings of a non-nuclear carrier and up to eight escorts. It is planned to enlarge these ships with a new midships section, increasing their current fuel capacity by a third and also making room for munitions and refrigerated stores.

planned 20, on account of its inadequate cargo capacity, 120,000 barrels compared with the 180,000 of the 1950s-built *Neosho* class. In order to make the *Cimarrons* fully employable as AOs with the fleet it has been decided to jumboise them, bringing their cargo capacity up to 180,000 barrels. The first ship will be converted under the FY 1988 programme, followed by two in each of the FY 1989 and FY 1990 programmes.

Construction of a new class of ammunition ship (AE) to replace the 1950s-built *Nitro* and *Suribachi* classes is to start under the FY 1986 budget and continue at a rate of one ship a year to FY 1989. A new class of fast combat support ship (AOE) is to be built, starting with the prototype in FY 1986 and continuing with one a year in FY 1988-90; at least two more are likely to follow. Finally, the FY 1989 programme will include construction of replacements for the *Ajax*-class repair ships (AR).

Auxiliary ship conversions include that of the oceanographic research ship *Hays* (AGOR-16) into a sound testing barge as a replacement for the smaller *Monob I* (YAG). *Hays* will be used to test quietening techniques for surface ships. This project is planned for the FY 1986 programme. In FY 1987 it is planned to convert an as yet unidentified vessel into a missile range instrumentation ship (AGM) to replace the ageing *Redstone* (AGM-20). The capabilities of the Near Term Prepositioned Force (NTPF) will be further enhanced

by the conversion of two commercial Ro-Flo container ships into aviation logistics support ships (AVB). They will serve as self-sustaining aviation and maintenance ships, each carrying a Containerised Aircraft Intermediate Maintenance Facility. The first ship, ex-SS *Young America* (AVB-3), is scheduled for the FY 1985 programme, while the second, ex-SS *Great Republic* (AVB-4), will be in FY 1986.

Also destined for NTPF are the auxiliary crane ship (ACS) conversions. The first, *Keystone State* (ACS-1), has already completed conversion and is now being tried out in various exercises. A second conversion, approved in the FY 1982 programme at a cost of $29.8 million, is now under way. There are two more in FY 1985 (ACS-3/4), three in each of FY 1986 and 1987 (ACS-5/10), and one in FY 1988 (ACS-11). This programme is needed because a significant portion of the US merchant fleet is made up of container ships which

Mispillion is now nearly 40 years old. Commissioned in December 1945, she belongs to the T3-S2-A3 class of 16kt oilers, which were enlarged in the mid-1960s to carry 150,000 barrels. They are operated by Military Sealift Command in support of the fleet, and each has a civilian crew plus a 21-man naval detachment. (*US Navy*)

The 12 sister ships of the *Hamilton* and Hero classes (*Gallatin* illustrated) were completed for the US Coast Guard in 1967–72. Of 3,050 tons full load, they carry a helicopter, a 5in and several smaller guns, and six anti-submarine torpedo tubes, and have a speed of 29kt on a diesel/gas turbine powerplant. They typify the effective support that the Coast Guard could give the USN in a crisis. (*W. Sartori*)

cannot be unloaded without full port facilities. The crane ships would be used to unload other vessels in areas where such facilities are lacking or damaged. After the ACS and AVB conversions are completed the ships will remain on "reduced operational" status in US ports, manned by skeleton crews and ready to sail at 5–10 days' notice. They would be fully activated at intervals for training and exercises.

The eight SL-7 commercial cargo ships purchased for use by the NTPF are being converted into vehicle cargo ships (AKP) as the *Algol* (SL-7) class. Four conversions were authorised in the FY 1982 programme and four in FY 1984. Each AKR will be able to lift the troops and equipment of a full armoured or mechanised US Army division, or most of the equipment of two such divisions. The first of class, *Algol* (AKR-287), entered service on June 19, 1984, followed by two sister ships on June 30, 1984. *Algol* has already participated in NATO's Exercise Reforger. Like the AVBs and ACS, the AKRs will be maintained at reduced operational status until they are needed.

The final conversion programme of note is the transformation of two liquid natural gas tankers into hospital ships (AH) under the FY 1983 and 1984 programmes. Cost per ship is $200.0 million. While *Mercy* (AH-19) will be assigned solely to the NTPF, *Comfort* (AH-20) will also be available for fleet use. The required medical staff will be drawn from shore medical facilities. *Mercy* is scheduled to complete her conversion in October 1986 and *Comfort* hers in July 1987.

As the shipbuilding and conversion programmes progress, many new items, such as the TACTASS (SQR-19) sonar, Captor mine, Standard (SM-2) surface-to-air missile and Vertical Launch System (VLS) for missiles, are under development or just entering fleet service. Thus the US Navy is not building new ships only to equip them with old systems and weapons. Indeed, the various budgets referred to earlier also include many millions of dollars for the development of new systems.

Admiral Thomas Hayward, then Chief of US Naval Operations, said in 1980: "We are a one-and-a-half-ocean Navy doing a three-ocean job." As President Reagan's second term gets under way, the US Navy has reached two-and-a-quarter-ocean status and looks set fair to complete its recovery during the next four years.

US Navy strength 1981/1984

Ship type	1981*			1984*		
	Atlantic	Pacific	Building	Atlantic	Pacific	Building
Submarines						
SSBN	31	7	8	31	4	7
SSN	42	34	23	56	38	18
SS	—	5	—	—	3	—
Total	73	46	31	87	45	25
Aircraft carriers						
CVN	2	1	2	2	2	3
CV	4	5**	—	5†	4	—
Total	6	6	2	7	6	3
Surface combatants						
BB	—	—	—	1	1	—
CGN	6	3	—	3	6	—
CG	7	11	2	9	11	12
DDG	21	16	4	23	14	—
DD	24	19	1	16	15	—
FFG	7	6	32	25	17	14
FF	29	30	—	25	28	—
Total	94	85	39	102	92	26
Patrol combatants						
PHM	1	—	5	6	8	8
PG	2	—	—	—	—	—
Total	3	—	5	6	—	—
Mine warfare ships						
MCM	—	—	—	—	—	5
MSO	3	—	—	3	—	—
Total	3	—	—	3	—	5

Ship type	1981*			1984*		
	Atlantic	Pacific	Building	Atlantic	Pacific	Building
Amphibious warfare ships						
LCC	1	1	—	1	1	—
LHD	—	—	—	—	—	1
LHA	2	3	—	2	3	—
LPH	4	3	—	4	3	—
LPD	6	7	—	6	7	—
LSD	6	7	—	5	6	4
LST	9	10	—	9	9	—
LKA	1	1	—	2	3	—
Total	29	32	—	29	32	5
Auxiliaries						
AD	5	4	3	5	4	—
AE	5	5	—	5	7	—
AFS	3	4	—	3	4	—
AGDS	—	1	—	—	1	—
AGF	2	—	—	2	—	—
AO	2	1	5	5	2	—
AOE	2	2	—	2	2	—
AOR	3	4	—	3	4	—
AR	1	3	—	1	3	—
ARS	3	3	—	3	2	4
AS	9	3	1	9	3	—
ASR	4	2	—	4	2	—
ATS	1	2	—	1	2	—
AGSS	1	—	—	1	—	—
AVM	—	1	—	—	1	—
AVT	1	—	—	1	—	—
Total	44	41	9	45	43	4
Naval Fleet Auxiliary Force (manned by Military Sealift Command)						
T-AE	—	1	—	—	1	—
T-AF	1	—	—	1	—	—
T-AFS	—	—	—	2	1	—
T-AGOS	—	—	3	1	1	9
T-AK	2	1	—	2	—	—
T-ARC	2	1	1	2	2	—
T-ATF	4	3	2	3	4	—
T-AO	6	7	—	5	6	4
Total	15	13	6	16	13	13
Naval Reserve Force						
DD	12	4		1	—	
FFG	—	—		1	1	
FF	—	—		4	2	
MSO	13	9		9	9	
LST	1	—		1	1	
LKA	1	2		—	—	
AE	—	2		—	—	
ARS	1	—		1	1	
ATF	2	3		2	2	
Total	30	20		19	16	
Sub-totals	297	231	92	314	247	81
Total active ships	528			561		

* As of January 12, 1981, and July 31, 1984, respectively. ** *Coral Sea* (CV-43) employed as contingency carrier. No air wing attached. † One unit always undergoing SLEP refit.

US Navy shipbuilding FY 1985–89

Class/Type of ship	1985	1986	1987	1988	1989
Shipbuilding					
Ohio-class fleet ballistic missile submarine (SSBN)	1	1	1	1	1
Los Angeles-class submarine (SSN)	3	4	4	4	4
New submarine (SSN)	—	—	—	—	1
Ticonderoga-class guided missile cruiser (CG)	3	3	3	2	2
Arleigh Burke-class guided missile destroyer (DDG)	1	—	3	5	5
Wasp-class multi-purpose amphibious assault ship (LHD)	—	1	—	1	1
Whidbey Island-class dock landing ship (LSD)	2	2	2	—	—
Modified *Whidbey Island*-class dock landing ship (LSD)*	—	—	—	2	2
Avenger-class mine countermeasures vessel (MCM)	4	4	1	—	—
Cardinal-class minehunter/Sweeper (MSH)	—	4	4	4	4
AOE-5-class fast combat support ship (AOE)	—	1	—	1	1
AE-36-class ammunition ship (AE)	—	1	1	1	1
AR-24-class repair ship (AR)	—	—	—	—	1
Henry J. Kaiser-class oiler (T-AO)	3	3	3	3	2
Stalwart-class ocean surveillance ship (T-AGOS)	3	3	—	—	—
AGS-39-class survey ship (AGS)	2	—	—	—	—
Conversions/Reactivations/Modernisations					
Multi-purpose aircraft carrier Service Life Extension Programme overhaul (SLEP) (CV-62/63)	1	—	1	—	—
Iowa-class reactivation/modernisation (BB-64)	—	—	1	—	—
Amphibious transport dock Service Life Extension Programme overhaul (SLEP) (LPD-4 class)	—	—	1	2	3
Cimarron-class jumboisation (AO-177 class)	—	—	—	1	2
AGM-24-class missile range instrumentation ship (T-AGM) conversion	—	—	1	—	—
AG-195-class sound testing barge conversion**	—	1	—	—	—
AVB-3-class aviation logistic support ship (T-AVB) conversion	1	1	—	—	—
Keystone State-class auxiliary crane ship (T-ACS) conversion	2	3	3	1	—

Figures correct to July 31, 1984. * Formerly called LPDX. ** Replacement for *Monob I* (YAG). *Hayes* (AGOR-16) to be converted.

***Keystone State*, first of the Near Term Prepositioned Force's auxiliary crane ships.**

MoD reorganisation: a personal perspective

Admiral of the Fleet Lord Lewin

The need for close co-operation between the services to ensure their efficient joint performance is an ever-recurring lesson of history. This was re-emphasised by the experience of the inter-war period and of the Second World War, when the part to be played by air power in future warfare was first evaluated in theory and then dramatically demonstrated in practice. Never again will wars be fought by armies and navies, operating in their separate environments; air power has introduced a third dimension. There is now virtually no foreseeable military operation that does not involve at least two of the services, and most involve all three.

The consequent need for close inter-service co-operation requires a command organisation to match it. But it was left to our United States allies in the Second World War to introduce us to the concept of a supreme commander, responsible for the whole conduct of a campaign, with sea, land and air deputies to advise him on particular single-service aspects. This form of organisation was applied to every major campaign from the invasion of North Africa in December 1942 onwards, in both the European and Pacific theatres, and is now universally accepted as the right pattern.

Yet after the Second World War the British national command organisation immediately reverted to the pre-war arrangement of three commanders-in-chief, with their headquarters sometimes separated by as much as a thousand miles or more and each accountable directly to his parent Ministry in Whitehall. A gesture towards co-operation was made by the institution of regional defence co-ordination committees under civilian chairmanship, but they depended on consensus and had little or no power. It was not until Admiral Mountbatten, the only British officer with wartime experience of supreme command, again reached high level after reverting post-war to the rank of rear-admiral that unified command was introduced, first in the Middle East, with headquarters in Aden, then in the Far East with headquarters in Singapore. Although these commands have now disappeared, the unified-command concept is the foundation of the NATO military organisation. For many years all solely British operations, together with our remaining overseas garrisons in Cyprus, Hong Kong, Belize and the Falklands,

have been the responsibility of a Commander British Forces. Calling when necessary for single-service advice, he commands all assigned units and is responsible directly to the Chief of the Defence Staff in Whitehall.

The Ministry of Defence is responsible for the successful conduct of operations and for the armed forces' being adequately prepared, equipped and supported, a prerequisite of high morale and confidence. If unified command is right for the conduct of operations, then the Ministry of Defence should work in the same way. But once again the British were slow off the mark after the war. During the conflict co-ordination of the three

Marshal of the Royal Air Force Sir William Dickson, pictured here as an Air Vice-Marshal, served as chairman of the Chiefs of Staff Committee during 1956–59 before becoming the first Chief of the Defence Staff. He was succeeded by Earl Mountbatten. (*IWM*)

107

The first Chief of the Defence Staff after the establishment of MoD (1963–5), Admiral of the Fleet Earl Mountbatten of Burma. He was the only British officer to have held supreme command in a theatre, Southeast Asia, during the Second World War. His experience there of the diverse requirements of all the armed services of the Commonwealth and the other Allies and of the intelligence and sabotage organisations served to reinforce his views on the need for an integrated ministry. (*IWM*)

Mountbatten to break the mould. In 1962, as Chief of Defence Staff (CDS), he determined to achieve more power for central policymakers by unifying the single-service Ministries into one Ministry of Defence. How to do it? Just to toss it into the ring as a proposal for debate would have engendered months if not years of acrimonious argument, with victory for the strong and emotional single-service interests probably inevitable. It was first necessary to get support for the proposition from Prime Minister Macmillan and Defence Minister Thorneycroft. This Mountbatten did privately, consulting no-one else, and both Prime Minister and Defence Minister were convinced. Next the Prime Minister appointed two retired officers, General Ismay and Lieutenant-General Jacob, to study the need for better co-ordination of defence policy and to make proposals for an improved central organisation. Ismay had been Churchill's Chief of Staff throughout the war, and Jacob had been Secretary of the War Cabinet. Two officers more experienced in the higher organisation of defence it would have been difficult to find.

Ismay and Jacob did their work quickly, and in a concise report which is a model of clarity and wisdom they put forward three broad options: the status quo,

Lord Lewin, Admiral of the Fleet and the only Chief of the Defence Staff (1979–82) to have held that post during a period of sustained conflict. It was during the Falklands campaign that the necessity for a far closer understanding between the three services became evident, not only at Ministry level but also in the operational area. (*IWM*)

single-service Ministries was in the hands of a powerful Prime Minister who also doubled as Minister of Defence. But, the war over, the Prime Minister relinquished direct responsibility for defence. The Admiralty, War Office and Air Ministry remained large and influential in their own spheres, each having a Minister with a seat in Cabinet. A Minister for Co-ordination of Defence was appointed, but he had virtually no staff and limited access to essential information, and as a result there was no powerful voice speaking for defence as a whole.

Successive Ministers of Defence expressed their dissatisfaction with this imbalance of power, but the single-service lobbies were strong, both in Parliament and in the country. In the years immediately after the war many people identified closely with one service or another. There were votes in the Army, Navy and Air Force but not in nebulous "Defence," and there was no strong political impetus for change.

Again, it took the vision and experience of Admiral

which they did not recommend; a unified Ministry of Defence, absorbing the Admiralty, War Office and Air Ministry but with separate service staffs and a strong central co-ordinating staff within it; or a completely unified Ministry of Defence with divisions responsible for policy, operations, logistics, personnel, equipment and intelligence, and covering all three services. They thought that although this organisation should be the ultimate aim, it would be too big a change to make in one step. They therefore recommended the middle course, but urged that this should be announced as a transitional phase until the ultimate was achievable.

Ministers did not waste time. Approval for the unified but federal structure was soon announced, but no decision on the more far-reaching changes was made. Staffs then hammered out the details, the new Ministry was born on April 1, 1964, and the Admiralty, War Office and Air Ministry ceased to exist as separate entities.

Mountbatten, uniquely equipped to be the architect of this change, had achieved probably more than any other man might have. But he had failed to reach the degree of centralisation that he believed desirable. Only in the intelligence area was he successful, with the

Admiral of the Fleet Lord Hill-Norton, who after a series of senior appointments in the Ministry, including First Sea Lord and Chief of the Defence Staff (1971–73), served as chairman of the NATO Military Committee. He too has misgivings about the reorganisation (*IWM*)

The now Field Marshal Lord Carver, who experienced the need for service co-operation when he was Commander Land Forces Far East at the conclusion of Indonesian Confrontation in the mid-1960s. Chief of Defence Staff during 1973–76, he has expressed reservations about the proposed reorganisation. (*IWM*)

institution of the fully integrated tri-service and civilian Defence Intelligence Services. In the new Ministry the single-service staffs, headed by their chiefs of staff, retained their identities and a powerful position relative to the centre. Thus they were able to block virtually all attempts at further evolutionary change, particularly in the area of an objective military input to defence policy and programmes.

The underlying urge towards further change was demonstrated by the ad hoc committees that were regularly set up to study and report on various aspects of the organisation. Most made some reference to the need to strengthen the centre's contribution to decision making, but little change was made. The Defence White Paper of the Labour Government in 1970 even went so far as to declare an intention to abolish single-service Ministers and to strengthen the position of the Chief of Defence Staff. Before this was implemented, a general election in July brought in a Conservative administration which naturally enough did not implement these proposals – at least, not until 11 years later!

This same period, starting in the middle 1960s, saw a succession of "defence reviews," all aimed at reducing

Marshal of the Royal Air Force Lord Cameron, who after a distinguished flying career and a period in the Ministry, culminating as Chief of the Air Staff, was Chief of the Defence Staff during 1977–79. His criticisms of the reorganisation, mainly concerning service morale, are answered here by Lord Lewin. (*IWM*)

prepare a paper or study an aspect of defence policy without first getting COS agreement to the terms of reference. While the responsibilities of the COS Committee for advising Ministers on all aspects of defence policy and strategy were fully set out in the "Little Green Book" on the organisation of the Ministry of Defence, which also contained the detailed terms of reference for the CDS and all the principal officers of the Central Staff, no similar directives existed for the single-service Chiefs of Staff.

These officers had a difficult, some might say an impossible, task. On the one hand, each had risen to become the professional head of his service, with ultimate responsibility for the service's performance on his shoulders. In the Ministry he led a powerful single-service staff who looked to him to be the champion of their cause, the presenter of their case. On the other hand, he was required to contribute to collective advice on defence policy which, particularly in the fields of resource allocation and equipment priority, might be in conflict with his own service's interests. As Professor Michael Howard put it in 1970, "It would be as reasonable to expect that a sound economic policy would

Admiral of the Fleet Sir Edward Ashmore, who has also served as Chief of the Defence Staff and First Sea Lord. Before that, his appointment as Assistant Chief of the Defence Staff, concerned with his own speciality of communications, came at a time when new methods in this field were demonstrating the problems of inter-service co-operation. (*IWM*)

spending on defence as a proportion of public expenditure as a whole, a standard political preoccupation in eras of continuing peace. The Healey review of 1965–66, which resulted in the cancellation of the replacement strike carriers for the Navy and of three major new aircraft projects for the Royal Air Force, set the pattern. This and each successive review, together with the normal conduct of business, underscored the problem of developing forceful, objective military advice in an organisation in which the principal contributors had divided loyalties.

The fountainhead of military advice was the Chiefs of Staffs (COS) Committee. The Chief of the Defence Staff, as chairman, was charged with tendering the collective advice of the committee. Only if the Chiefs of Staff disagreed was he directed to represent their separate views, and to tender his own advice. CDS had no staff of his own, other than a small, non-executive briefing staff. The Central Staff, manned from all three services, was responsible to the CDS only in his position as the chairman of the COS Committee. For example, the CDS could not direct the Central Staff to

emerge as a result of bargaining between the principal trade unions."

Small wonder, although few of the participants of the time would be likely to admit it, that the Chiefs of Staffs Committee fell into disrepute and disrepair. In the days when we still had the operational and administrative problems of overseas commitments the Chiefs met regularly every Tuesday afternoon, with the Vice-Chiefs dealing with residual business on Thursdays. By the late 1970s and early 1980s the Chiefs were meeting about once or twice a month and the Vice-Chiefs not at all. In the struggle for agreement, so that advice should be "collective," the result was too often the lowest level of compromise, while the horse-trading between the principal contestants, conducted by the Central Staff or the COS Secretariat, took an inordinate time. Other parts of the Ministry could get their advice to a Minister more quickly and more crisply and thus it often carried more weight. An indication of the diminishing contribution of the Chiefs of Staff was the infrequency of their attendance at meetings of the Cabinet's Defence Committee. Understandably, Ministers looked askance at being almost outnumbered by a deputation of five from the Ministry of Defence (Secretary of State, CDS and the three Chiefs of Staff), particularly when, if there was any military business, it would usually be handled by the CDS alone. As the years passed, invitations to the Chiefs became rare: I can recall perhaps less than five in the whole 1978–81 period.

For me the culmination of years of frustration came with the Nott Defence Review of 1981. John Nott was a man in a hurry, events moved at too great a speed for the COS organisation and the single services were fully preoccupied in defending their own positions. The Central Staff were unable to make an effective contribution, and once again we failed to grasp the essential problem of overall defence priorities. In the aftermath, encouraged by the shared feelings of the majority of the officers on the Central Staff, I resolved to propose changes aimed at strengthening the military input to the major questions of defence policy.

Together with my senior advisers on the Central Staff, I developed proposals based on five essential principles which, without formally consulting my COS Committee colleagues, I put to the Secretary of State. Briefly, the five principles were:
• The Chief of Defence Staff should become the principal military adviser to the Government in his own right, not just as chairman of the Chiefs of Staffs Committee.
• The COS Committee would become the forum in which the CDS would seek the advice of the Chiefs of Staff, but would no longer have collective responsibility.
• The Chiefs of Staff would remain the professional heads of their own services, responsible for morale and efficiency, and for advising on all aspects of defence

Field Marshal Sir Edwin Bramall, current Chief of the Defence Staff.

policy as well as their own single-service matters.
• The Central Staff would be responsible to the CDS in his own right, not as chairman of the Chiefs of Staffs Committee.
• A Senior Appointments Committee would be formed, consisting of the CDS and the Chiefs of Staff, to oversee the promotion and appointment of all three and four-star officers, and of two-star officers in certain key posts.

The vital importance of this last principle may not be self-evident. Previously promotion and appointment of these senior officers was a matter for each service, with the appointment of three and four-star officers solely in the hands of the Chief of Staff. Although in theory the Chief of Defence Staff could nominate officers for important posts on the Central Staff in the Ministry of Defence and for rotational posts outside it, in practice, because of the need to keep a balance between the services, he had little choice. An additional disadvantage was the fact that the future career of an officer serving on the Central Staff lay with his own service, and it was not unknown for one who had served the interests of defence outstandingly well to be denied his deserved reward of further good appointments or promotion.

After some discussion, during which the Chiefs of Staff were able to voice their objections and misgivings about the diminution of their power, the principles were endorsed by the Secretary of State and approved by the Prime Minister. John Nott chose a rather obscure method of announcing the changes and the bringing them into force. Perhaps remembering the chorus of criticism from Tory backbenchers that the abolition of the single-service Ministers had attracted the year before, he conveyed the decision in a letter to the chairman of the All-Party Parliamentary Defence Committee on February 10, 1982. As a consequence, it attracted little attention, although it was probably the most significant change in the organisation of the Ministry of Defence since its formation in 1964, and certainly the most important change in the position of the Chiefs of Staff for over 50 years.

By a remarkable stroke of fate, six weeks later the new organisation was subjected to the test of war. This is not the place to discuss in detail the higher conduct of the unexpected and totally unforeseen operations in the South Atlantic, but I believe it is widely acknowledged that the machinery for crisis management worked well.

As CDS I attended every meeting of the small "War Cabinet". It would have been unnecessary and inefficient for the Chiefs of Staff to attend as well, as would have been axiomatic under the previous regime. The Chiefs of Staffs Committee was the focus within the Ministry of Defence for the exchange of information and the co-ordination of advice, serving the Secretary of State, the Permanent Under-Secretary (PUS), who was responsible for public relations, and the CDS. Outside the committee I was able to consult Chiefs of Staff individually rather than collectively, and single-service Chiefs of Staff accompanied me to the War Cabinet when an important matter affecting their service was being discussed. All Chiefs of Staff were present when major decisions were debated.

Although the new division of responsibilities proved satisfactory in this operational crisis, no-one would claim that this presages equal success with the much more recalcitrant problems of defence priorities and resource allocations. But the CDS now had a Central Defence Staff under his own control, unfettered by the need to seek unanimity or consensus. The Central Staff would of course continue to rely on the Naval, General and Air staffs for professional single-service inputs, and the need for continued two-way freedom of access between the staffs was self-evident. Preoccupation with the South Atlantic campaign impeded progress on a restructuring of the Central Staff aimed mainly at combining responsibilities for the defence programme and equipment priorities under a Deputy CDS. The details were worked out in conjunction with my successor, Field Marshal Sir Edwin Bramall, who had been a supporter of my proposals. I handed over my responsibilities to him on the day that these changes within the

Earl Mountbatten and Field Marshal Sir Richard Hull. The latter had the daunting task of taking over from Mountbatten in 1965. He was succeeded in 1967 by Marshal of the Royal Air Force Lord Elworthy, the pattern of the three services taking turns in the top job thus being set. (*IWM*)

Central Staff were implemented. By the turn of 1982–83, apart from Field Marshal Bramall, all the principal dramatis personae had changed: the three Chiefs of Staff and the Permanent Under-Secretary were new, while Michael Heseltine had succeeded John Nott as Secretary of State.

In March 1984 Mr Heseltine published a discussion document containing proposals for a further evolutionary development in the organisation of the Ministry of Defence. Building on the strengthened position of CDS and the Central Staff achieved two years earlier, it proposed the combination of the Central, Naval, Air and General staffs, together with some elements of the Defence Secretariat, into a fully unified and integrated military/civilian Defence Staff. This was to supply advice to all parts of the Ministry, including the Chiefs of Staff. At the same time, an Office of Management and Budget was to be formed, combining the finance divisions of the secretariat responsible for administering the single-service "target headings". In the past the separate existence of these divisions had tended to encourage the illusion that there were still Navy, Army and Air Force budgets, rather than a single Defence budget.

These proposals were a major and logical step in the further evolution of a unified Ministry of Defence in which the single-service influence would be properly balanced by true defence interests, an aim of the 1964 changes which had not yet been achieved. After much discussion within the Ministry and in other places, including a debate in the House of Lords in which four former Chiefs of Defence Staff took part, the final details of the new organisation were published in July in the White Paper *The Central Organisation for Defence* and will be implemented on January 2, 1985.

Criticism of the changes has centred on three main concerns:

1 The transfer of the bulk of their staffs to the Defence Staff will render the Chiefs of Staff less able to contribute considered advice; although responsible for executing policy, they will be increasingly divorced from responsibility for making it. In fact they will have full use of the Defence Staff in the way that CDS and the Central Staff had freedom of access to the Naval, General and Air staffs in the past. The position is just reversed. The CDS Committee will remain the forum in which the military advice on defence policy is debated. The CDS is required to take into account the views of the Chiefs of Staff and to ensure that they are properly represented, and it would be a foolish CDS who failed to do this. The individual Chiefs of Staff retain their right of direct access to the Secretary of State and to the Prime Minister if they feel that their views are being dangerously ignored. All the safeguards are there. But there is a genuine belief that the transfer of staff may have gone too far, and this was the principal concern that the Chiefs of Staff represented to the Prime Minister when the changes were being considered. They have been given an undertaking that this aspect in particular will be reviewed after a year's experience of the new organisation.

2 There is a suggestion that the apparently diminished status of the Chiefs of Staff will have an adverse effect on service morale. It is difficult to take this seriously. At the sharp end the fighting serviceman looks up the chain of operational command towards a distant commander-in-chief for inspiration and leadership, not to Whitehall. Those with high ambitions will see the Chiefs of Staff as still the professional heads of their services, fully responsible for fighting effectiveness, management, overall efficiency and morale, but serving in a Ministry in which the military trumpet has a more certain sound. I think that the morale of our fighting forces is unlikely to be disturbed by organisational changes within the Ministry of Defence.

3 Lastly, there is the fear that in the new structure the Civil Service will have a predominance of power over the military, particularly through the new Office of Management and Budget. Careful reading of the White Paper shows that – compared with the previous organisation, which had the military staffs and the civilian secretariat in entirely separate branches accountable to the CDS and the PUS respectively – the reverse is the case. The new organisation will see a much closer integration of the military and civilian elements in combined branches in both the Defence Staff and the OMB. In the Defence Staff responsibility will pass through the Vice-Chief of Defence Staff (VCDS) mainly to the CDS, but also to the PUS for the political and parliamentary aspects of its work. Two particular examples are illustrative. Whereas before the influential civilian Deputy Under-Secretary (Policy) headed an entirely civilian staff and was accountable to the PUS, in future he will head an integrated civil/military part of the Defence Staff, accountable through the VCDS to CDS for the military aspects of his work. Another important senior civilian, the Chief of Public Relations, previously accountable solely to the PUS, will now be accountable jointly to the PUS and CDS.

Any organisation depends for its effectiveness on the quality and motivation of the people within it. It would be foolish to claim that this or that arrangement of responsibilities or accountabilities in a Department of State as large and as complex as the Ministry of Defence is exactly right. Circumstances alter, weaknesses emerge, adjustments have to be made. Because the performance of the machine depends on people and their attitudes, change takes time. Judging from the appointments already announced, the key figures in the new organisation have been chosen with care and discrimination. They will need to tackle their great new responsibilities with patience and goodwill. I, for one, wish them every success.

Can the Royal Navy carry the Trident load?

Capt John Moore RN

The Royal Navy is currently embarking on a number of major projects which are essential to the proper discharge of its duties to the nation. The majority of these have their origins within the Ministry of Defence, although the most controversial and expensive, the Trident programme, is the result of a decision by a small Cabinet group. Successor to Britain's Polaris submarine-launched deterrent, this system now promises to be so costly that there is a growing clamour for an alternative, varying from outright cancellation, through the refurbishing of Polaris boats and the use of cruise missile submarines, to the somewhat unsatisfactory "let's do it cheaper" approach. Setting aside the rights and wrongs of the concept, what is the price likely to be, how is this to be spread, and what effect will the programme have on the Navy as a whole?

The price given by official sources is in the region of £8.7 billion. Other estimates vary up to £12 billion, vastly greater, particularly when one realises that the

Heading picture Invincible, invaluable in the Falklands campaign and seen here against the background of another British outpost, Gibraltar. This class was first designed in 1961 as helicopter cruisers. When the 1966 Defence Review resulted in the axing of the Royal Navy's aircraft carrier programme the plans were resurrected and modified to allow for Sea Harrier V/STOL aircraft. Once built, *Invincible* was almost sold to Australia. But then came the Falklands War, in which she proved vital to the British victory. Today every means of providing seaborne air power, fixed or rotary-wing, is desperately needed. (*Michael D. J. Lennon*)

whole of the bill will be borne by the Naval Vote. Even if the official figure is correct, Trident must have a major impact on other programmes. The government's claim that only three per cent of the defence budget will be expended on Trident is misleading. This figure has been reached by amortising the cost over the building period and service life of the four Trident submarines, whereas spending actually peaks in the second half of the construction phase and then falls to the annual running cost. The four-boat Trident programme will make its heaviest demands during the late 1980s and early 1990s. If this timetable can be held the situation may be bearable. But if design changes, shipyard disruption and technical difficulties conspire to cause delays and further cost increases the problems will be very severe.

As it is, the programme will hold up the construction of more fleet submarines of the *Trafalgar* and future classes. The target of 18 nuclear attack boats is attainable but there is little room for error or delay. The best means of overcoming this problem would have been the re-opening of the nuclear building stream at Cammell Laird in Birkenhead, but this is reckoned to be too expensive.

The sensible decision to back up the nuclear fleet submarines with a class of non-nuclear boats has resulted in the Type 2400, the first of which is about to be ordered. Experience suggests that this design is not only too big for the tasks to be allocated but will also be too costly. Several other criticisms of this class have been offered in the past, drawing scant response from the designers. One such was that the boat was underpowered, and it is now interesting to learn that from No 5 onwards boats of this class are to be further enlarged to accommodate more powerful engines. At a time when the West Germans are within four years of testing their first submarine equipped with fuel cells, this approach appears little short of antediluvian.

Tireless, third of the *Trafalgar*-class SSNs, was launched on March 17, 1984. Although this is a highly efficient design, the projected force of 17 fleet submarines (including earlier classes) is inadequate. Moreover, the building rate will be cut as the Trident boats begin to occupy the building slips at Barrow.

Sceptre is one of the six *Swiftsure*-class SSNs, commissioned between 1973 and 1981. With the USSR producing an average of 11 submarines of various classes every year, this is a measure of the problem that NATO faces. (*John G. Callis*)

Bristol was the only one of the Type 82 destroyers to be built. Designed around the Sea Dart GWS 30 SAM system, these ships were intended to act as escorts for the aircraft carriers of the CVA-01 design, cancelled in the 1966 Defence Review. This loss of role, plus their high cost of building, resulted in the cancellation of the remaining Type 82s. In 1979–80 Bristol was fitted with flagship facilities. (Michael D. J. Lennon)

▲ Fife was one of the later County-class DDGs, built in the 1960s at the urging of Lord Mountbatten. The first of class was paid off in 1976, seven years before she was due for disposal. By 1985 all but three had been sold or broken up. (Michael D. J. Lennon)

▼ Liverpool is one of the Type 42 Batch 2 destroyers. The first of the class, Sheffield, was lost off the Falklands, followed by Coventry three weeks later. The need for improved close-range weapon capability thus revealed has led to the inclusion of a number of 40mm and 30mm guns at the expense of the ship's boats. (W. Sartori)

Alacrity was one of eight ships built to the Vosper Thornycroft Type 21 design; two were subsequently sunk off the Falklands. Type 21 was a private design much modified by the Ministry of Defence. In service these ships proved to lack longitudinal strength at deck level, a shortcoming cured by the installation of heavy steel reinforcing straps in the hull. (*W. Sartori*)

Charybdis is one of the second group of the originally 26-strong *Leander* class. Ships of this group were given an extra two feet of beam compared with their predecessors. In place of the 4.7in turret *Charybdis* and four others have been fitted with four Exocet SSMs and a sextuple Seawolf launcher. Four earlier ships of the class carry towed-array sonars, the extra topweight requiring the removal of the air surveillance radar, the replacement of the boats by a Searider inflatable, the lowering of the Exocet mountings and torpedo tubes, replacement of the 40mm guns with 20mms and the addition of a twin 20mm aft. All this was needed to cater for an extra 70 tons on the lowest weather deck. (*W. Sartori*)

Boxer is first of the Type 22 Batch 2 frigates. Like Batch 3 of the Type 42 destroyers, the Type 22 design has had to be lengthened after the first four ships. Six Type 22 Batch 2 ships are to be followed by the three-ship Batch 3. Although those who criticised the lack of gunnery armament in the original Type 22s were told to "climb into the missile age", the two 20mm guns in Batches 1 and 2 have been augmented by a 4.5in, two 40mm singles and two twin 30mm guns in Batch 3. (*W. Sartori*)

Surface ship construction is now centred on the Type 22 Batch 2 and 3 frigates. The latter ships, the first two of which were ordered in December 1983, show a return to sanity in their armament. The Falklands campaign prompted a radical change to their gun fit: in place of the two 40mm guns in the earlier ships, provision was made for a 4.5in, two 40mm, four 30mm and two 20mm guns. The lessons of the Mediterranean and Pacific campaigns of 40 years earlier had been relearned at great expense.

The Type 23 frigate, originally to be a "cheap" design, has grown until it is now only marginally smaller than the original Type 42 destroyers, although the Batch 3 ships of the latter class are now over 50ft longer than the Batch 1s. In the Type 23 a 4.5in gun is to be complemented by a close-in weapon system and two 20mm guns. Main armament comprises eight SSMs, vertical-launch Sea Wolf SAMs and two Lynx or EH101 helicopters. With two Spey gas turbines and electric drive, this class will be closer in capability to the current first-line frigates than was originally expected.

In response to the urgent need for greater numbers in the fleet, it is now planned to build a class of smaller ships. Commercial shipbuilders have been invited to tender, and it is to be hoped that the big battalions of Bath and British Shipbuilders will not snuff out other worthy consortia. Memories of the first trials of the

One of the basic requirements behind the design of the *Peacock*-class patrol ships was an ability to withstand typhoon conditions. *Peacock* rolled violently during trials, however, which suggests that she and her four sisters may have problems as they patrol the typhoon-prone waters of Hong Kong. (*W. Sartori*)

Abdiel commissioned in 1967 to act both as a support ship for MCM vessels and as a minelayer. She is the only RN ship with the latter capability. (*W. Sartori*)

Cattistock is the third of a planned 12 ships of the Hunt class of minehunters/sweepers. The Hunts have their origins in the early 1960s, when the use of GRP hulls were recommended. The first of class commissioned in March 1980. Average cost per ship is £30 million. (*Gilbert Gyssels*)

been quoted. Meanwhile, the first five of a class of 12 steel-hulled minesweepers have been commissioned. These, the "River" class, are intended for RNR divisions and will be employed on deep sweeping in offshore approach routes.

To put the force levels given above into perspective, it should be remembered that the mine-clearance tasks for Operation Neptune on June 6, 1944, required 287 vessels of various types, some 24 more than the current total holding of all the NATO navies combined. The COOP programme of the USN, based on fishing ves-

Peacock-class patrol vessels for Hong Kong inspire hopes of a design that is very, very much better in almost every department.

The minesweepers of the "Ton" class were inspired by discoveries made during the Korean War, which finished in 1953. Thirty-one years later they still represent the bulk of the British mine countermeasures forces. Although the first plans for replacement of the Tons were initiated in 1962, the first of the "Hunt" class was not laid down until September 1975, when all but 37 of the original 118 Tons had been deleted. Twelve Hunts should be in service by about 1987. However, their price tag of over £30 million each prohibits a bigger programme, and in 1983 a design for a single-role minehunter was approved; as yet no cost has

Upton, although modernised in some areas, is typical of the very large Ton class of minesweepers. Since they were built in the 1950s these ships have served, and in some cases are still serving, in seven navies other than the RN. (*Gilbert Gyssels*)

119

This photograph of *Waveney*, first of the 12 steel mine-sweepers of the River class, emphasises her trawler-type hull. These 890-ton ships will be allocated to RNR divisions, which will find them quite a change from the present equipment, the 440-ton Ton-class sweepers.

A drawing of the new Single-Role Minehunter, designed as a cheaper back-up for the very expensive Hunt class. (*Vosper Thornycroft*)

Reliant (ex-*Astronomer*) **was converted for use off the Falklands and returned to her original condition when the campaign was over. She was then acquired by the MoD and converted to carry Arapaho containerised aviation support facilities.** (*Royal Navy*)

sels fitted with side-scan sonar, would be of little use in Great Britain, with its steadily dwindling fishing fleets.

In the vital area of fleet support, over the last two years the Royal Navy has begun to show signs of an originality which has been missing for too long. The conversion of the container ship *Astronomer* into the Arapaho-type RFA *Reliant* proved that this concept is acceptable if not ideal. More important is the conversion of MV *Container Bezant*, now in hand. Intended to replace RFA *Engadine*, approaching her 20th birthday, this ship will carry six Sea King helicopters and be capable of operating 12 Sea Harriers. Though this project represents a major step forward, new construction remains the most effective way of providing for naval needs. But until irrational government attitudes to

naval construction are overcome, such expedients will remain necessary.

More such conversions would go a long way towards meeting the fleet's requirement for more V/STOL and rotary-wing aircraft platforms. A careful analysis by independent naval architects has shown that a container ship of reasonable size can provide not only accommodation for aircraft but can also answer the need for support of amphibious operations. Had the Nott plan not been frustrated by the Falklands campaign, the Royal Navy would now have no means of transporting that fine and highly trained intervention force, the Royal Marines. The 1981 Defence Review, so hastily and inefficiently cobbled together, took no account of the vital role of these troops, who would presumably have waited, all 7,700 of them, on the jetties of Scotland while civilian ferries were diverted to transport them. Offshore command and control is essential to the success of an amphibious landing, the exit from the beaches and the subsequent deployment. Facilities for this must be built in: no instant conversion of a ferry would be acceptable. Replacements for *Fearless* and *Intrepid*, both heroines

Fearless and her sister LPD *Intrepid* were due for deletion under Defence Minister Nott's master plan for defence until the Falklands conflict brought them back into the forefront, where they have stayed. They proved to be invaluable in that short war and provision for their replacement is long overdue. (*Michael D. J. Lennon*)

of the Falklands and 20 years old in the near future, should by rights be on the slips. The controversial stop-go defence policies of the present government have nullified any such plans by the naval staff, so alternatives must be found.

The Royal Navy has at last accepted the need for a multi-purpose replenishment tanker designed to pro-

vide not only fuel but other necessary stores. The "eggs in one basket" argument is irrelevant. A theoretical force of four tankers and four supply ships needs the same number of escorts as eight multi-purpose ships, and one of the latter needs fewer escorts than a tanker and a supply ship.

Arakan is one of a pair of modern logistic landing craft (LCL) built for the Royal Corps of Transport. Apart from these craft and the two RN-manned LPDs, British amphibious capability consists of six LSLs manned by the Royal Fleet Auxiliary, five small landing craft and eight 100-ton lighters manned by the RCT, and a total of 42 LCPs, LCMs and LCVPs. (*Gilbert Gyssels*)

A Royal Navy decision to make use of the handy and effective oil-rig support ships was long overdue. Seen here is *Sentinel* (ex-*Seaforth Warrior*), one of three such vessels acquired for Falklands patrol duties. (*W. Sartori*)

Equally effective is the use of converted oil rig supply vessels as patrol and repair ships. These signs are all encouraging to those who appreciate the vital role of the Royal Navy as an element in the conventional deterrence of war.

Herald is one of the four ocean survey ships which, with four coastal survey ships and four inshore craft, make up the totally inadequate force available to the Hydrographic Service. (*Michael D. J. Lennon*)

Tidespring is the oldest of the four large fleet tankers of the Royal Fleet Auxiliary. Five support tankers and five small fleet tankers complete the line-up of ships dedicated to keeping the RN fuelled at sea. This evolution is necessary every three or four days, with the result that the RFA's tankers had to be extensively supplemented by merchant vessels during the Falklands campaign. (*Michael D. J. Lennon*)

123

Britain's Merchant Navy: down by the bow and sinking fast

Nigel Ling

Although fully 96% of all United Kingdom trade is seaborne, only a quarter of it is carried in ships flying the Red Ensign. As Britain's merchant fleet shrinks, so too do its significant foreign earnings and, even more important, the nation's ability to defend itself. Britain's survival has depended entirely on seaborne supplies throughout two world wars, and the outcome of both conflicts hinged on a regular supply of stores and munitions from west to east across the Atlantic. There is every reason to believe that the outcome of any future major conflict would be decided in the same area.

In 1982 the merchant service underlined its importance by rapidly mobilising ships to form the greater part of the Falklands Task Force. The continuing decline in available tonnage leaves little doubt that had the internal politics of Argentina allowed President Galtieri to delay his foray into the Malvinas until 1985 or 1986 he could have invaded with impunity, for the

shipping needed for an 8,000-mile-range reoccupation would not have been available.

The decline in available tonnage has been so rapid – 40% in the last seven years – that if ship disposals continue at the present rate the fleet will cease to exist by 1993. There are several reasons for the withering away of the Merchant Navy. The world recession has

Heading picture The container ship *City of Durban*, 53,800 tons gross and built in West Germany in 1978, can carry about 2,500 containers at 21kt. Vessels of this type are now carrying much of the cargo previously handled by conventional general cargo ships. Measuring 260m long and 32m in the beam, and with a draft of 13m, they are restricted by their size as to the number of ports they can visit. They are also gearless and thus totally dependent on shore installations for cargo handling. (*Michael D. J. Lennon*)

reduced the amount of freight to be carried, resulting in increased competition and ever-lower freight rates, to the point where high-cost British ships can be sailing full and yet still losing money.

The state-supported and controlled Eastern-bloc operators, with their determination to earn foreign currency and increase their sphere of influence, are quite happy to undercut accepted rates by up to 40%. They have no fixed costs in the form of insurance, loan or depreciation charges, a subsidy if applied to their fuel, and crew wages are only a fifth of Western levels. Despite protectionism by many nations their penetration of the traditional cross-trading routes continues to increase.

That same protectionism, reserving trade for home-flag vessels, has heavily hit British owners, who have traditionally cross-traded. Many nations have made all their coastal trades and sections of foreign trade the sole preserve of their own vessels. Britain has not responded, and her own waters remain something of a free-for-all. For example, Norway, whose merchant service has declined in a similar way to that of Britain, has reserved all oil rig supply work in the Norwegian sector of the North Sea for Norwegian flag vessels, but the UK sector is supplied by vessels flying not only the British but also the Panamanian, Dutch, German, Liberian, US and Norwegian flags. On top of

that, the March 1984 budget abolished the free depreciation and various capital allowances introduced in 1965, further increasing the operating costs of the British-flag owner.

As well as having high-cost crews, British-flag vessels are manned by a trade union that operates the closed-shop system. Union requirements have ensured that manning levels for British ships are significantly higher than those of many foreign competitors. Dis-

Earl Godwin, built in 1966 as the Swedish *Svea Drott*, raised the Red Ensign in 1975, when she entered Sealink service. The 68 passenger ships and ferries currently British-registered range from large liners like *Queen Elizabeth 2* and *Canberra*, employed primarily on cruises, to ferries like the *Earl Godwin*, engaged in short sea and Channel crossings. (*Michael D. J. Lennon*)

The Soviet 16,000-ton deadweight cargo vessel *Svoboda*. This 19kt turbine ship was built 20 years ago as part of a 25-ship class. Equipped with two 60-ton derricks and five-ton cranes serving all hatches, these self-sustaining vessels are typical of the large numbers of Eastern Bloc ships that have achieved such deep market penetration worldwide. (*Michael D. J. Lennon*)

The Greek-flag *Pleias* began life in 1963 as the British *Silver-leaf*. This traditional five-hatch general cargo vessel is one of many sold into Greek ownership. (*Michael D. J. Lennon*)

ruption in the form of a month-long strike took place in 1981 during a critical period in the run-down of the fleet, and the refusal of crews to carry coal and more recently nuclear waste on some classes of ship means that the union is now reserving the right to choose the cargo it is prepared to carry.

A large part of the decline in British tonnage has affected traditional self-sustaining general cargo shipping, much of which has been sold into Greek ownership. Increasingly large amounts of cargo are now carried in large cellular container ships which do not have their own handling equipment. Their size restricts them to the very small number of ports equipped with the large "portainer" cranes required to handle containers from such ships. With the number of such cranes in the country being measured in tens rather than hundreds, Britain's cargo-handling capability is even more vulnerable to enemy action than the ships. Port facilities are particularly susceptible to sabotage, the long-term immobilisation of a portainer crane requiring little more than a well aimed sledgehammer.

The United States, aware of the number of vessels that are not self-sustaining, is currently converting eleven ships to be maintained in reserve as auxiliary crane ships. They would be used to discharge container ships in ports which lacked the necessary facilities or had had them destroyed. No other nation has yet shown such foresight.

Lack of a total maritime policy and indifference on the part of the government to the plight of the merchant service means that there is no prospect of a recovery by British-flag shipping in the foreseeable future. With its increasing penetration of world trade and the decline of Western fleets, the Eastern bloc will eventually be in a position to disrupt Western economies simply by withdrawing all of its vessels to home waters.

With the British fleet now below 20 million tons, the time has come to arrest the decline by implementing a comprehensive maritime policy. The point of no return is rapidly approaching: beyond it lies only the prospect of a nostalgic ceremony in the 1990s when the Red Ensign is hauled down for the last time.

British merchant fleet: world ranking

Year	Gross tons (×1,000)	Ranking
1976	32,923	3rd
1977	31,646	3rd
1978	30,896	4th
1979	27,951	4th
1980	27,135	4th
1981	25,419	5th
1982	22,505	6th
1983	19,121	7th

Note: All figures from Lloyds Information Services.

The 22kt refrigerated cargo vessel *Imilchil* is a Moroccan-flag ship which trades regularly with the United Kingdom. Third World and emerging nations, and those without a seagoing tradition, are increasingly building up their merchant fleets and reserving domestically produced cargo for home-flag vessels. Morocco is aware of the contribution that a merchant fleet can make to the national economy and has now registered 261 ships. (*Michael D. J. Lennon*)

The Norwegian anchor-handling tug *Sistella*. While the Norwegian North Sea oil sector is reserved exclusively for Norwegian-flag vessels, the British sector remains a free-for-all in which vessels like the *Sistella* can compete for charters. (*Michael D. J. Lennon*)

British merchant fleet: composition

Type	Number	Deadweight tons	Gross tons
Dry cargo	275	1,877,902	1,299,866
Container	141	2,404,881	2,232,695
Tankers	264	14,350,728	8,315,768
Bulk carriers	244	15,210,227	8,371,737
Passenger and ferries	68	121,070	488,041

1 Comprises all vessels of over 1,000 tons deadweight built since 1967.
2 Includes Hong Kong-registered vessels not listed in table above.
3 Correct to September 7, 1984.

Principal merchant fleets of the world

Country	1976 (Gross tons ×1,000)	1983 (Gross tons ×1,000)
Liberia	73,477 (1)	67,564 (1)
Japan	41,663 (2)	40,752 (2)
Greece	25,032 (5)	37,478 (3)
Panama	15,631 (7)	34,666 (4)
USSR	20,668 (6)	24,549 (5)
USA	14,909 (8)	19,358 (6)
United Kingdom	32,923 (3)	19,121 (7)
Norway	27,943 (4)	12,230 (8)
China	3,589 (10)	11,554 (9)
Italy	11,077 (9)	10,015 (10)

Figures in brackets in columns 2 and 3 indicate world rankings.

These photographs show general cargo vessels owned by the Bank Line. A family company with long traditions, Bank Line has found its cross-trading routes increasingly vulnerable to penetration by operators from the Eastern Bloc and the emerging nations. As a result, its fleet has shrunk in recent years from 50 ships to just 12. MV *Laganbank* (above), now the Greek-registered *Amphion*, was built in 1978 and sold to foreign-flag owners after only three years' service. MV *Birchbank* (below), now the Liberian-registered *California*, was built in 1973 and also sold in 1981. (*Bank Line*)

▲ MV *Tenchbank*, 12,200 tons gross, is one of a six-ship class built in 1978–79. Five remain in Bank Line service, while the *Ruddbank* still flies the British flag, trading as the *Romsey* in the ownership of Lamport and Holt. Each with one 60-ton, one 35-ton, one ten-ton and five 22-ton derricks, these ships are completely self-sustaining; container capacity is 370 TEU. These modern and versatile general cargo ships are direct descendants of the traditional dry cargo vessels that served Britain so well during the two world wars. (*Bank Line*)

▼ MV *Meadowbank*, now ten years old and seen here berthed alongside a strategically vulnerable container crane, belongs to another six-ship class. *Corabank* was sold in 1984 to foreign buyers, while the remaining five operate a round-the-world service via the South Pacific and Australasia. With two 15-ton cranes capable of operating in tandem, these vessels are self-sustaining for containers in Nos 3 and 4 holds. In addition, an 80-ton derrick serves No 3 hold and the remaining derricks all have a ten-ton capacity, allowing the class to operate without any fixed port facilities. (*P. N. Ling*)

Russia's battle with the northern ice

Dr Terence Armstrong

In the autumn of 1983 the Western media carried brief reports of a protracted struggle to free dozens of merchant ships trapped by freak ice in the waters of the Soviet Union's sub-Arctic Northern Sea Route. Soviet publications and broadcasts have since revealed many details of an icebreaking campaign of unparalleled difficulty.

An early freeze-up in 1982 caught many ships on the Yenisey and Lena rivers. The spring of 1983 seems to have come late, and heralded a short and cold summer. It was reported on August 4 that autumn had already started on "the polar islands" (not specified), and that summer had lasted only 17 days. In September about 70 ships, together with eight icebreakers, were in or near the port of Pevek. In view of the weather in the previous weeks, an early end to the season was expected. An improvement in early October prompted

an attempt to get as many ships as possible either out of the area or, in some cases, into Pevek. Unfortunately the improvement was temporary. Northerly winds brought a sharp drop in temperature, fast ice along the north coast of Chukotka started forming two weeks earlier than usual, and 51 ships were caught in the ice. This figure seems to be the most reliable out of the many quoted, which range from 22 to 90.

Ships were caught at six locations (A-F on map) and at least 13 icebreakers were involved, including the three nuclears, *Lenin*, *Leonid Brezhnev* (formerly *Arktika*) and *Sibir'*. This force probably represented every available icebreaker. On about October 6 some 20 ships, including two tankers and the icebreakers *Kapitan Sorokin* and *Leningrad*, were caught in the vicinity of Kosa Dvukh Pilotov off the north coast of Chukotka (A on map). Some of the ships were westbound for

This article is based on a paper first published in 1984 in *Polar Record* 22 (137).

Heading picture   Russian merchantmen caught fast in the ice off north-eastern Siberia. (*Novosti*)

Pevek. *Leonid Brezhnev*, *Yermak*, *Admiral Makarov* and *Vladivostok* arrived and released nine of them (presumably eastbound) in about mid-October and took them to the ice edge to the east, whence they could get to the Bering Strait. One ship, *Nina Sagaydak*, a small freighter built in East Germany in 1970, was holed and sank on October 8, though all hands were saved. This was the only total loss of the season.

Other ships were released in the following days, but by October 22 there were still five freighters stuck in that locality, with *Kapitan Sorokin* and *Leningrad* still trying to help. *Leonid Brezhnev* reappeared and on October 25 the freighter *Amguyema* was released after two days' work by the three icebreakers. Another of the trapped vessels, the tanker *Kamensk-Ural'skiy*, could be moved only two cable lengths in eight hours by the combined efforts of the three icebreakers. *Leningrad* then lost power in two of her eight diesels and retired eastwards, escorting some of the other freighters, and was herself helped at times by *Leonid Brezhnev*. Other ships were taken northwards towards Ostrov Vrangelya, where the ice was slightly easier, since the island offered protection from the north. There they joined another group which formed later (C).

Meanwhile, about 80nm to the north, in the Chukchi Sea (B), there was another group which included the icebreakers *Vladivostok*, *Magadan* and *Kapitan Khleb-*

nikov. On about October 8 one of the freighters, *Kolya Myagotin*, a sister ship of *Nina Sagaydak*, was pierced by ice, which made a 3m × 1m hole in the hull. Desperate efforts were made to save the ship, though an order to abandon her had been given, and she finally reached Provideniya on the Bering Strait on October 23. Others of this group seem also to have escaped eastwards.

The group sheltering to the south of Ostrov Vrangelya became important in the later stages of the rescue operation. The ships seem to have been chiefly inbound with freight for Pevek, and there was clearly no intention of abandoning these voyages. The tanker *Urengoy* was taken to Ostrov Vrangelya from location A by *Admiral Makarov* and *Kapitan Sorokin* at the end of October, and five other ships were left there, drifting in the ice, with *Vladivostok* and *Kapitan Khlebnikov* in attendance. *Leonid Brezhnev* then came out from Pevek and took *Urengoy* back there, where her cargo of oil was evidently badly needed.

It was now early November and little daylight was left. *Okha*, carrying cargo trans-shipped from one of

The Soviet Union's Northern Sea Route. Letters A–F on the inset map indicate the position of icebound freighters (see text).

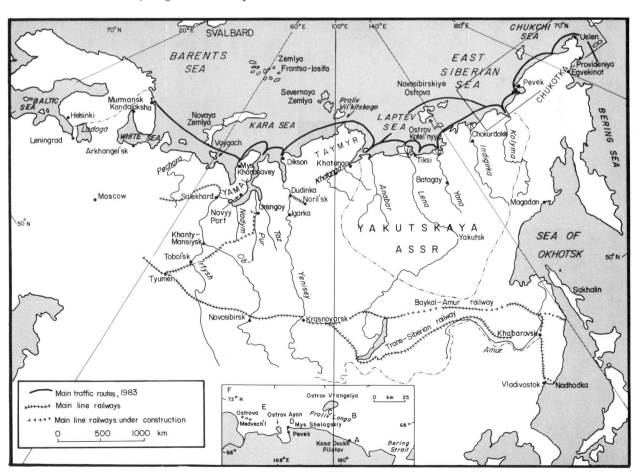

the immobilised ships, reached Pevek from C on about November 5. On November 6 *Vladivostok* and *Yermak* were trying to bring to Pevek four of the ships remaining in this group (others were awaiting escort eastwards). The four including *Kamensk-Ural'skiy* and *Amguyema*, which had previously had a very difficult time at A. But this move was suspended until the ships could be joined by *Leonid Brezhnev*, which had been delayed by heavy ice pressure. The group were now the only freighters still in trouble out of the 51 originally caught. *Kamensk-Ural'skiy*, escorted by both *Leonid Brezhnev* and *Sibir'*, reached Pevek on November 14 after a very difficult passage. The other three got there two days earlier. All four were unloaded in quick time, and by November 17 some were on their way back, together with another tanker, *Samotlor*, which had come in from the west.

Other groups had been caught farther west. One, consisting of seven ships, was off Mys Shelagskiy (D), just north of Pevek. Another, of four ships, lay near the Ostrova Medezh'i (E), and a third, of three tankers and four dry cargo ships, was off the mouth of the Indigirka (F). In addition there were nine ships waiting in Pevek to go westwards. The group at F were the most fortunate. They were released on about October 21 by the icebreaker *Kapitan Nikolayev*, coming from the west. A few days later *Sibir'*, also coming from the west, met the convoy and took it across the Laptev Sea. *Lenin* joined them and there were no more problems. It seems likely that the group at E joined this convoy, which was said to number 15 as it passed through Poliv Vil'kitskogo on about October 28, and the ships reached western termini by November 5. The group at D had a hard time, however, and was moving very slowly westwards on October 28, escorted by *Krasin* (which had mean-

while come in from the west) and *Kapitan Dranitsyn*. They had to await the arrival of *Lenin*, which left the first convoy at Dikson and returned eastwards with *Sibir'*, *Murmansk* and *Kapitan Nikolayev*. They brought with them the tanker *Samotlor*, bound for Pevek from Arkhangel'sk. Interestingly, the route followed at this stage of the season was northabout round the Novosibirskiye Ostrova.

Around November 5 *Samotlor*, with two nuclears in attendance, was making about 48nm a day north of Ostrov Kotel'nyy. *Krasin*'s convoy had by then safely crossed the Laptev Sea and reached Dikson on November 7. *Samotlor* battled on, now with three icebreakers at hand, and finally reached Pevek on November 15.

No ship was now stuck in the ice, but a number were facing a very difficult voyage back to home ports. It had been decided on about October 27 that eight freighters and two port icebreakers should winter at Pevek. The remaining three tankers and four dry cargo ships set out about November 17–22 under powerful escort.

The nuclear-powered icebreaker *Sibir'* played a key role in the fight to rescue the trapped cargo ships, shuttling virtually non-stop for the duration of the campaign.

The diesel-powered *Yermak* worked well with the three big nuclear icebreakers, *Sibir'*, *Lenin* and *Leonid Brezhnev*.

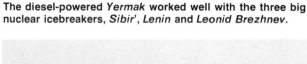

Magadan, sister ship to Mudyug (illustrated), took part in the desperate effort to save Kolya Myagotin, which had been holed by ice. (Wärtsilä)

Kapitan Khlebnikov, of the improved Kapitan Sorokin class, was designed for operations in shallow North Siberian deltas at temperatures as low as −50°C. She is fitted with Wärtsilä bubbling equipment. (Wärtsilä)

There was indecision as to whether the ships should go eastwards, where the most difficult ice had been, or westwards, where conditions were easier but the distance much longer. The eastwards option also offered the opportunity, recently exploited, of sheltering south of Ostrov Vrangelya. *Sibir'* accordingly took two ships there and she returned to bring up the others, helped by *Yermak*, *Admiral Makarov* and *Krasin*, although the latter had originally been ordered west. *Lenin* took one freighter west, once again rounding the north side of the Novosibirskiye Ostrova. *Leonid Brezhnev* waited for the final freighter, *Kamensk-Ural'skiy*. The decision

on which way to go seems to have been delayed until the last moment, and it is not altogether clear what it was. No further difficulties were reported, and Pacific-based freighters were probably able to return there. But the final, remarkable, convoy of *Kamensk-Ural'skiy* and four icebreakers appears to have gone westwards.

Difficulties of this scale and severity have never been encountered before, and there is an evident desire in the Soviet Union to learn as many lessons as possible from them. A deputy minister of the merchant fleet, A. V. Golbodenko, quoted in *Vodnyy Transport* of December 10, 1983, made the following points:

• It was realised in July-August that things would get difficult in the eastern sector. To that end, repairs to *Leonid Brezhnev* were speeded up, new SA-15-class freighters were sent to the Arctic as soon as they had been delivered, schedules were rearranged, and some freight was sent to Egvekinot in southern Chukotka for onward transport by road in order to relieve the sea route.

• Recently introduced ship types performed well. The nuclear icebreakers were of decisive importance, the *Yermak* class worked well in harness with the nuclears, and the SA-15 freighters (*Noril'sk* class) showed themselves very reliable. These last are capable of independent movement in ice up to one metre thick, and were often used as icebreakers, for which they earned much praise. Criticism was reserved for the *Samotlor*-class tankers, which experienced difficulties, and for certain ports which lacked the equipment needed to handle the SA-15s efficiently.

• Ships' crews did extremely well, but the blameworthy people were often the shippers, who delivered goods to port late and thus disrupted schedules and caused late arrivals in the Arctic.

Other sources reveal that the damage to ships was significant. Besides the loss of *Nina Sagaydak* and the severe damage to *Kolya Myagotin*, 30 ships were damaged, including *Leonid Brezhnev* (propeller), *Igarka* (steering), *Pioner Uzbekistana* (unspecified), *Amguyema* (propeller shaft), *Arkhangel'sk* (steering), *Georgiy Sedov* (steering), *Leningrad* (engines), *Pioner Rossii* (propeller) and *Yermak* (unspecified). But there was no loss of life.

The enforced routing of ships to ports many thousands of miles from their bases obviously caused severe disruption of freighting plans over the ensuing months. It must have been several months before a Vladivostok ship, obliged to go to Murmansk, was able to return to Vladivostok.

The *Pravda* correspondent at Pevek was critical of certain aspects of the operation. He demanded whether the conditions alone were to blame, and went on to note inaccurate ice forecasts, delays due to late loading and, in particular, "morally and physically worn-out ships". He urged the creation of a central authority which could exercise real control, and cited the Chief Administration of the Northern Sea Route (*Glavsevmorput'*) as a good example of what was needed (it was abolished in the 1960s), However, there appear to have been no senior dismissals as a result of the episode.

Ye. Tolstikov, vice-chairman of the State Committee for Hydrometeorology and Environmental Control and himself a very experienced polar man, revealed that although the Arctic and Antarctic Research Institute's long-term forecast, issued in March, had been wrong, the Institute had issued correct warnings in July and August about the anomalously large size of the ice clusters in the East Siberian and Chukchi Seas. The unusually severe conditions should therefore have come as no surprise. He went on to draw the following lessons: nuclear icebreakers can only make their full contribution if ice behaviour is fully understood, and this is not yet the case; powerful icebreakers require strong freighters – it is no good putting ships like *Nina Sagaydak* behind nuclear icebreakers; when onshore winds are predominant, shipping lanes further from the coast should be sought; finally, year-round operations in the eastern sector are a realistic goal, but in order to attain it there must be an improvement in both scientific and organisational work.

The episode will have to be taken into account when plans are made for the year-round working of the whole route, due to begin in 1990 at the earliest. There is some recognition of the fact that the climate is deteriorating and has been for some time, and though technological advances have until now offset this, the time may come when they can no longer do so. A broadcast on December 22, 1983, supports this view, stating that freight for the far north-east would in future be routed where possible from the west rather than from the Soviet Pacific coast, thus avoiding the area of Proliv Longa (between Ostrov Vrangelya and the mainland), where much of the trouble started. The ice reconnaissance service, hitherto seasonal, is to be year-round, and will be supported with Ka-32 helicopters.

There is no doubt that the rescue operation was carried out with skill and determination, and what might have been a major disaster ended with all freight deliveries successfully completed and relatively minor damage to ships.

Submarine incursions: Sweden fights back

Carl Bildt

When the Swedish Government handed over its strongly worded protest note to the Soviet Government on April 26, 1983 – following the publication of the report of the Submarine Defence Commission the same day – many expected to see an end to Soviet submarine incursions into Swedish waters. The commission had made a careful study of the pattern of incursions since 1980, with special emphasis on the major incident in the Horsfjärden area – the main base of the Swedish Navy – in October 1982. Its conclusions were clear: responsibility for the 1980–1982 incursions must lie with the Soviet Union, and so did that for the dramatic activity in the Horsfjärden area. Moreover, the latter was in the opinion of the commission only part of a wider operation in the Stockholm archipelago by at least six different submarines, three of which were midget craft of hitherto unknown type[1].

Naturally the Soviet Union denied the Swedish charges. They were called an "unfriendly act," and the Soviet Government even went as far as asking the Swedish Government to punish those responsible for the Submarine Defence Commission report. Swedish–Soviet relations reached their lowest level since the shooting down by the Soviet Air Force of a Swedish Air Force Catalina over international waters in the Baltic in 1952.

According to the commission, the incursions represented "the preparatory phases of military operational planning". This conclusion was reached after a

Hugin-class FAC operating with a helicopter. In addition to their normal surface attack weapons and the M83 anti-submarine grenade launcher, these craft carry depth charges and a Simrad SQ-3D/SF sonar.

lengthy discussion in which other possible motives were tested against what was known of the actual behaviour of the intruding submarines. It was found that only a programme of operational preparations could explain the pattern observed during 1982.

Submarines are useful for a number of tasks during a full-scale attack on a country. One of those mentioned by the commission was the landing of raiding parties intended for quick strikes against command and control installations and other sensitive parts of the defence system. In such cases the ability to reach the target areas clandestinely is of the utmost importance. Given the difficulties associated with navigation in the skerries and shallow bays of the archipelagoes along the Swedish Baltic coast, peacetime training would be necessary to ensure that these demanding but crucial tasks could be performed in case of war.

It is known that the Soviet Union expanded its diversionary forces during the 1970s. According to published reports, the diversionary brigades associated with each of the Soviet fleets include midget submarines on their strength.

Following publication of the commission's report, during the remainder of 1983 submarines were sighted along different parts of the Baltic coast of Sweden. The Commander-in-Chief of the Armed Forces (ÖB) reported 25 certain incursions by foreign submarines

during the year, plus 38 probables. These were the highest numbers ever recorded[2].

It would be unwise to draw too many conclusions from these figures. Even if they represent a 10 per cent rise in comparison with 1982 figures, this could well be the effect of increased alertness on the part of both civilian and military observers. Even so, certain of these incidents are worth special attention.

During both the spring and summer submarines were observed in the Gulf of Bothnia, exploring waters of obvious military importance adjacent to the Swedish defence lines along the Swedish–Finnish border and in the increasingly significant Sundsvall area. Swedish naval defence in the Gulf of Bothnia has traditionally been weak. It has always been assumed that foreign naval vessels could be prevented from penetrating the strait between the Swedish mainland and the Finnish island of Åland, since they would have to cross either Swedish or Finnish territorial waters. Obviously these restrictions have not been respected, and submarines showed in 1983 that they were able to operate in the Gulf of Bothnia in a way that invalidates both Swedish and Finnish defence planning.

It also became obvious that the submarines could penetrate not only the peacetime base areas of the Swedish Navy but also its wartime locations along the entire Baltic coast. In doing so they seem to have paid special attention to base defensive systems. The pattern of submarine operations in 1983 thus supported the conclusions of the Submarine Defence Commission.

Most of the incursions have been observed during the summer months. This might however be more of a reflection of the number of people present in the Swedish archipelagoes during different times of the year than of the submarines' actual cycle of operations.

Swedish Defence Commission drawing, showing "foreign" naval divers operating in a Swedish permanent minefield. The method being used, incorporating a measuring line, is outmoded by normal Western practice. The drawing is based on a report delivered by an inspector of coastal fortifications in September 1983.

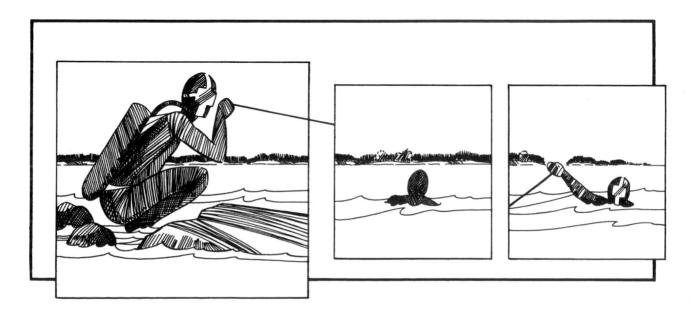

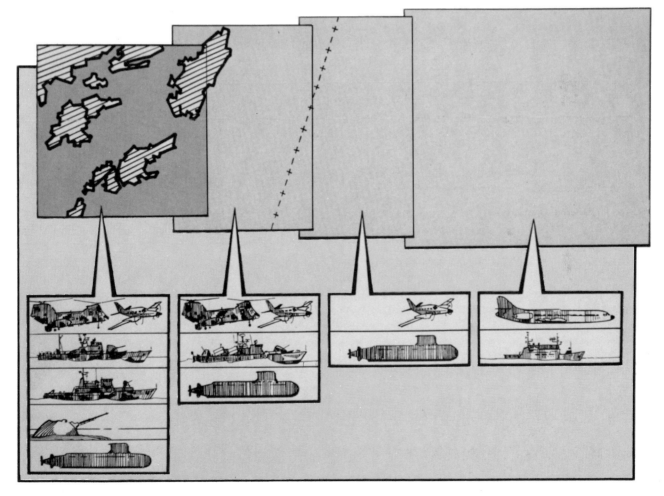

This illustration from the Swedish Navy magazine shows Sweden's successive lines of defence against submarine intrusions. From the right: ships and Caravelle patrol aircraft fitted for electronic intelligence-gathering; submarines and light aircraft fitted with forward-looking infra-red; the addition of Hkp 4 helicopters and coastal patrol craft; the inshore phase, in which the aircraft and submarines are joined by *Hugin*-class FAC and *Landsort*-class minehunters. The shore battery shown would be used by the Navy against surfaced submarines.

Late in the evening of February 9, 1984, the installations guarding the main entrance to Karlskrona in Southern Sweden reported the passage of a submarine into the inner part of the archipelago. Over the next few days further observations left no doubt that a foreign submarine had managed to penetrate the inner areas. Karlskrona is, after Horsfjärden, the Swedish Navy's most important base area. The ensuing search, which went on for nearly a month, was the largest ever undertaken by the Swedish armed forces. However, the intruder managed to escape, and probably did so at a fairly early stage of the Swedish operation.

The Karlskrona incident was important in that it deepened Western understanding of the submarine operations. While the Horsfjärden incursion had brought proof of the use of both midget and conventional submarines, the Karlskrona incident brought evidence of the use of divers in association with the midget submarines.

Divers had in fact been observed earlier. In late September 1983 an inspector at one of the coastal fortifications in the Stockholm archipelago had a clear view of divers working on one of the permanent minefields blocking the entrances to the important parts of the archipelago. It was concluded that they must have been foreign military divers. No surface vessels were seen in the vicinity, but as the area has been visited frequently by foreign submarines, it seems likely that the divers came from an underwater craft.

Divers were spotted several times in Karlskrona. In one case a diver was seen going ashore on an island forming part of the chain between the inner basin and the sea, crossing the island and disappearing into the water on the other side. Independent civilian experts who have checked these observations have concluded that they are correct. In his report on the Karlskrona incident, published on May 7, 1984, ÖB agrees: "The activities have included larger submarines outside the skerries as well as smaller vehicles and divers in the skerries area."[3]

At no time has it been possible to produce conclusive evidence as to the nationality of the intruders, and ÖB

has been most careful to avoid naming suspects. However, ÖB has reported that midget submarines the same as those observed in Horsfjärden have since been seen at a number of locations along the Swedish coast. The details of their superstructure are now so well known to the Swedish Navy that sightings can now be sorted with a high degree of certainty into midget submarines and other craft. It has also been deliberate policy to keep the particulars of the midget submarine secret, making it much easier to discriminate between correct and erroneous reports.

The additional knowledge gathered since the publication of the Submarine Defence Commission report tends not only to support its conclusions but also suggests that the main responsibility for the incursions lies with the diversionary forces attached to the Soviet Baltic Fleet. The appearance of divers might have come as a shock to a large part of the Swedish public, but in fact it was hardly surprising in view of the commission's analysis of motives and missions.

The summer of 1984 brought a new wave of incursion reports. Some came from military units, but most were the work of civilian observers. ÖB was due to report on these sightings in October 1984[4].

The new pattern of submarine operations against Sweden was first noticed by the Swedish military authorities in 1980, and in 1981 the "Whiskey on the rocks" incident brought the reality of this new threat before a wider audience. Four years have passed since then. Regardless of what happens during the next year or two, the "submarine crisis" is thus not a passing phenomenon, without wider implications for the security of Northern Europe. The operations demonstrate

---

Sjöormen-class submarine *Sjöbjörnen*, displacing 1,400 tons dived and commissioned in 1969. Submarine operations in Swedish coastal waters are complicated by the many layers of water of different density and temperature.

Hkp 4 helicopter with dipping sonar. All ten of these aircraft are based at Horsfjärden.

Type 42 torpedo on an Hkp 4 helicopter. This 400mm-diameter torpedo can be fitted for wire guidance and passive homing and is launched without a parachute. Designed for use against surface ships or submarines, it has a normal warhead of about 50kg; the version shown here is the "incident torpedo" with a reduced charge.

Fast attack craft of the *Hugin* class (*Vale* shown here) are now fitted with an M83 anti-submarine grenade launcher ahead of the 57mm/L70 Bofors gun.

Observation posts such as this have some value but, being obvious, are easily circumvented by attack swimmers.

Sea Owl (*Sjöugglan*), an underwater surveillance device capable of laying charges. Although intended primarily for minehunting, this system would also be of value if a submarine of any size were detected.

a high degree of skill on the part of the submarine crews, and a disregard for political restrictions that indicate the importance attached to their results by the Soviet military authorities.

During the 1970s Sweden thinned out its anti-submarine forces as a consequence of an overall reduction in the number of its most highly trained military units. Shipborne ASW disappeared altogether, leaving just ten Hkp4 helicopters – Japanese-built Boeing/ Kawasakis fitted with French Alcatel dipping sonars and Swedish Philips fire-control systems – split between the Baltic and West coasts.

The ASW helicopters cannot cope with bottom-crawling submarines operating in the skerries. The submarines can hear a helicopter approaching, and can easily avoid detection by dropping to the bottom and waiting for the helicopter to break off to refuel. The helicopters remain very good for open-sea operations against submarines which have to move as they try to attack surface vessels. They are also the most important quick-reaction element of the combined ASW system now planned.

The Submarine Defence Commission's report resulted in a crash programme to improve ASW capabilities. The new minehunters of the *Landsort* class, equipped with powerful bottom-scanning sonars, will be integrated into the planned ASW force. Sonobuoys and associated electronics are being bought and modified for Swedish use. Magnetic detection systems are being installed at key entrances. Fixed sonar systems are being planned. The new coastal corvettes of the *Stockholm* class, two of which are being built and four of which will be ordered in the next few years, will be fitted with VDS systems. New weapons are being developed, foremost among them being the m/83 depth charge, designed for use from the fast patrol boats now forming the core of the provisional ASW groups.

During 1983 the Swedish Navy reorientated its entire training programme in order to be able to support the permanent operation of ASW groups along the Baltic coast. Each consisting of a light aircraft, helicopters, a division of patrol boats, other surface vessels with sonobuoys and bottom-scanning sonars, and submarines for surveillance duties, the groups have introduced new standards of readiness, communications discipline and secrecy in the Swedish naval forces.

Over the next few years new equipment will be delivered to the Navy, while tactics are further refined. The coastal corvettes will form the nucleus of the ASW groups, making possible a lengthier search for conventional submarines outside the skerries area. New devices will increase the possiblity of detecting intruders inshore.

In spite of all this, the odds will be on the side of the intruders for some time to come. The extremely difficult hydrographic and water conditions of the Baltic, the skill of the adversary and the fact that he has managed to find a gap in Sweden's naval capabilities, all add up to a formidable task for the Swedish Navy over the next few years. Gradually, however, the gap will be closed. New equipment, new tactics, refined intelligence and a new awareness of the threat will gradually increase the risks associated with these incursions to levels that should be intolerable even to a superpower.

Notes

1 *Countering the Submarine Threat: Submarine violations and Swedish security policy*. SOU (Swedish Official Report Series) 1983:13. Ministry of Defence.
2 ÖB reports: *Ubatsincidenter sommaren 1983*, September 16, 1983, *Sammanställning ubatskränkningar hösten 1983*, December 20, 1983; *Incidenter 1983*, June 19, 1984.
3 ÖB report: *Ubatsincidenten i Karlskrona varen 1984*, May 7, 1984.
4 Press statement by the Defence Staff, August 15, 1984.

A recovery run for Swedish naval attack divers, probably the toughest and best trained unit in the armed forces.

A self-propelled, radio-controlled magnetic/acoustic mine clearance platform, which clearly has other applications. Normally unmanned, it is seen here carrying two safety crewmen on a demonstration run.

Soviet special forces at work in the Baltic?

Victor Suvorov

In the winter of 1939–40 the Soviet Union was taught a cruel lesson in Finland. The Red Army came up against two unforeseen obstacles. Firstly, the country's forests, mud, lakes and deep snow made it impossible to apply the most important principle of war, the timely concentration of forces against the opposition's most vulnerable spot. In fact there was no such decisive location: the enemy was everywhere and nowhere at the same time, and there was no continuous front against which to concentrate.

Secondly, the Finnish people were prepared to make any sacrifice to preserve their freedom. Finland is the only country in the world to have fought the Soviet Union and kept the enemy's tanks out of its capital. Soviet armour has been in Berlin, Warsaw, Bucharest, Budapest, Sofia, Prague, Belgrade, Riga, Vilnius, Tallin, Ulan Bator, Pyongyang, Kabul and once even in Tehran – but never in Helsinki. The lesson learned in Finland was swiftly applied. Within four months of the Winter War, the Soviet Union had seized three sovereign Baltic states – Estonia, Latvia and Lithuania – without firing a single shot or losing a single soldier.

The governments of these three countries were too afraid of a bloody war and did not share the Finns'

toughness, resolve and readiness to make sacrifices. Consequently, their people were forced to carry on an unaided resistance war which they eventually lost. In the end they forfeited their freedom and statehood and were forced to make more sacrifices than the people of Finland.

There is little scope for aggression in the Baltic region today. Finland is too strong – the Kremlin is very well aware of this – and Estonia, Lithuania, Latvia, Poland and East Germany are already under Soviet control. West Germany, Denmark and Norway are members of NATO, and to attack them would be tantamount to taking on the entire Alliance, including the USA. Thus there is only one target left: Sweden. This neutral country could be subjugated in one of two ways. Direct aggression, as against Finland in 1939–40, would cause the whole population under the leadership of the government to act in defence of their

---

Heading picture **Each Spetsnaz naval brigade has two or three battalions of frogmen.**

country. Sweden is better located than Finland in that there is no common border with the Soviet Union, making a direct assault much more difficult. This leaves the method used so successfully against Estonia, Lithuania and Latvia, which entails paralysing the government and depriving it of the ability to offer resistance at the decisive moment.

It must be emphasised that the prime target of the USSR is not the population but the government of the country. The populations of Estonia, Lithuania and Latvia made a stand, conducting armed resistance against the aggressor for a number of years. But their governments surrendered without a fight to become the first victims of Soviet expansionism. The same thing happened in Afghanistan. The people showed themselves ready to resist and even now are waging a heroic struggle, but the government gave in tamely to the Soviet Union's first use of special forces for the annexation of a country.

Why Sweden?

It would be a simple matter for the USSR to turn Western Europe into a radioactive wasteland. But to capture these rich economies largely intact would be far more difficult. A prerequisite would be the isolation of Europe from America. It would be essential to interdict and if possible halt the shipping of troops and armaments from the United States to Europe. In other words, Europe could only be seized (as opposed to destroyed) following direct action by the Soviet Navy in the Atlantic.

The offensive capability of the Soviet Navy is growing fast, but the Soviet high command has only limited forces at its disposal for active operations in the Atlantic. The Pacific Fleet is a long way away and has enough problems of its own. The Black and Baltic Sea Fleets are enclosed in land-locked seas, and their release into the deep oceans would necessitate major operations in the Bosphorus area and the Danish Straits. The 5th Squadron of the Soviet Navy is permanently stationed in the Mediterranean but lacks a base there and could be deprived of supplies at any time. Moreover, it would have little chance of fighting its way through the Straits of Gibraltar and into the open Atlantic. The Soviet high command can therefore rely only on being able to deploy the ships and submarines of the Northern Fleet into the Atlantic. But the Northern Fleet bases are situated north of the Arctic Circle, and to reach the Atlantic these ships and submarines have to carry out a long passage between the hostile coastlines of Greenland and Norway. Even if the Soviet Union were at some time to achieve parity with NATO in numbers of carrierborne aircraft, the West's bases in Britain, Norway, Greenland and Iceland would still give it air superiority in the Norwegian Sea. In this region the Soviet Union can only use heavy aircraft without fighter cover.

Let us put ourselves in the position of the Soviet admirals. There is no way of entering the Atlantic

---

Soviet warships attempting to escape into the North Atlantic would have to run the gauntlet of NATO anti-shipping aircraft like this Kormoran-armed Tornado of the German Marineflieger. (*MBB*)

unseen, which removes the element of surprise. The enemy has air superiority over a very long corridor, which would mean heavy losses before entering the Atlantic. It would be exceptionally difficult to support vessels in the Atlantic, since the Soviet bases are some 1,500 miles from Iceland and the supply ships would suffer heavier losses than naval vessels. The return voyage to Murmansk would be even more difficult. Vessels would have only limited quantities of fuel and ammunition, and any damaged ship would be faced by a very hazardous voyage. Air power apart, there would be an enormous threat to Soviet shipping from NATO surface ships and submarines deployed from the Norwegian fjords and northern British bases. How then can significant naval forces be deployed in the Atlantic?

If the Soviet Union were preparing itself for defence the problem would not exist, since the Red fleet has enough ships to defend its own shores. But the Soviet Union is making ready to mount a broad-fronted offensive operation in Europe, and this demands the intervention of the Soviet Navy in the Atlantic. Success in the Atlantic can however only be guaranteed if safe passage for ships and submarines into the ocean can be secured, if their appearance is sudden, if their lines of communication are not too stretched, and if both the outward and return voyages are covered by friendly aircraft. To achieve all this the Soviet Union must have at least one readily defended naval base in the south of Norway, well covered supply routes, and several airfields from which combat aircraft, including fighters, could operate over the North and Norwegian seas. The best place for such bases is Norway, and the easiest route for an assault on Norway lies across Sweden.

Paralysing the Swedish Government

The Soviet Union possesses one great foreign-policy advantage over the Western democracies: the absolute clarity of its ultimate aims, which are openly expressed and have remained unchanged for over half a century. Because this final goal is so clear and immutable the Soviet leadership is able to expend a long time preparing its operations. For example, the preliminaries for the invasion of Afghanistan were carried out over a period of 25 years. In the West there are always very convincing arguments against the belief that such preparations are for aggression, and when the deed has been done there is neither the time nor the means, apart from diplomatic protest, to react.

Time is on the side of any government which does not suffer the regular disruption caused by democratic elections. If a Western state is seen to risk losing its sovereignty, the government and population protest vehemently and are ready to defend their county by all

possible means. It is therefore much simpler to destroy a state's sovereignty by a process of slow, gradual strangulation which goes largely unnoticed and does not give rise to violent and simultaneous reaction. Thus in the case of Sweden the Soviet Union has opted for the well tried method of "slow aggression". Under this plan Sweden is being steadily persuaded that whoever can penetrate her territorial waters can also penetrate her territory.

When the Soviet submarine was stranded close to the naval port of Karlskrona in October 1982 the Swedish Government could have followed a hard or a soft line. The first called for the destruction of the submarine and its crew, which is the accepted Soviet action even in the case of civilian aircraft. If the Swedish Government had done this it would now have no problems with Soviet submarines, and Moscow would be going to great lengths to improve Soviet–Swedish relations. The Soviet leadership not only understands strength but also respects it. Any nation that betrays weakness, however, risks falling victim to the Soviet Union.

Alternatively, the Swedes could have gaoled the submarine captain for 15 years (as the Soviet Union did with American U-2 pilot Gary Powers) and thoroughly examined the vessel. If they had done so there would at least now be no question about what Soviet submarines are doing on the Swedish coast. But in the end Sweden effectively did nothing, letting the submarine go and confining itself to a diplomatic protest. A criminal can only react to a protest before the crime has been committed, however, and this course of action is little more than an open invitation to further incursions.

But it is still not too late for positive action. Soviet submarines often enter Swedish waters and the Swedes' objective should be to destroy one of them. This would be an unmistakable signal to the Soviet leaders that Sweden is prepared to defend its freedom. If this is not done, the provocation will intensify and the USSR will ultimately insist that the Swedish Government adopts a "friendly" posture towards the Soviet Union.

To resist such pressure the threatened country must give the Soviet Union the correct signals. The invasion of Afghanistan was certainly a grave error on the part of the Soviet leadership, but the Afghan authorites must also share some of the responsibility. If the latter had borne in mind the fact that the people would fight for their freedom, expelled the Soviet spies and not allowed the Soviet intelligence services to carry out "geological" surveys upon their territory, then the aggression would never have taken place. As it was, the Afghan Government continually displayed weakness, and the Soviet leadership considered that the people would be equally malleable. This was a mistake, one that is now being paid for by the people of Afghanistan. Does the Swedish Government want to see its country go the same way as Afghanistan?

If ever Sweden attacks a Soviet submarine in earnest, the Hkp 4 (CH-46) ASW helicopter will be in the vanguard. This example was photographed at a temporary landing ground on the outskirts of Stockholm. Depth-charge carriers can be seen below the national insignia.

The strengths of slow aggression

What are Soviet submarines actually doing in Sweden's territorial waters? There are various theories: they are surveying naval bases and obstacles; monitoring tests of new weapons; putting Spetsnaz sabotage groups ashore; provoking incidents and then analysing the Swedish Navy's subsequent tactics. While it is likely that all of these guesses are correct, there can be no doubt that there is yet one more purpose to the incursions: the erosion of Swedish sovereignty. Each violation of the Swedes' territorial waters is a deliberate strike at the sovereignty of a neutral state which for more than 250 years has participated in no war or conflict. The Soviet Union is clearly provoking one of the most peace-loving states in the world into open confrontation.

Operations against Sweden are run by the GRU, the Soviet military intelligence organisation currently headed by Army General P. I. Ivashutin. Directly responsible are the GRU's Directorates 1 and 5. The First Directorate is responsible for European strategic intelligence, excluding Great Britain. In Western Europe this directorate has 23 intelligence *residentura*s concealed in embassies and other official establishments. On the same territories there are also several illegal *residentura*s. Heading each *residentura* is a colonel or major-general, with support from officers of the

General Staff, each of whom is engaged in the active recruiting of foreigners. Foreign nationals are used for anything, from the propagation of disinformation to direct terrorism. Each officer, irrespective of the territory in which he operates, pays particular attention to citizens of Scandinavian countries.

The Fifth Directorate does not carry out independent operations abroad, but co-ordinates the activities of the 24 independent intelligence services of the Soviet fleets, groups of forces and military districts. Each of these independent services (RU) forms part of the parent formation's headquarters, and three of them – the Leningrad and Baltic military districts and the Baltic Fleet – are playing an active role in the cold war against Sweden. It is the Baltic Fleet RU that plays the key role.

The head of this service is a rear-admiral who is subordinate to the Chief of Staff of the Fleet, Vice-Admiral K. V. Makarov, who in turn is subordinate to the Commander of the Fleet, Vice-Admiral I. M. Kapitanets. In addition, the head of the RU is also under the control of the Fifth Directorate of the GRU. The GRU, KGB and other secret units are under the direct control of the Department of Administrative Organs of the Central Committee of the Communist Party, the current head being Nikolai Ivanovich Savinkin. Sometimes Western observers imagine, incorrectly, that the Central Committee and, above it, the Politburo exercise only political authority. In fact these two organisations direct every form of activity.

The Baltic Fleet RU comprises five departments. **Department 1** has officers on every Baltic Fleet vessel that puts out to sea. Officers with civilian cover are also to be found on merchant vessels; they visit foreign ports posing as merchant seamen or tourists. The department also controls all legitimate means of gathering information, including reconnaissance aircraft and ships, with the exception of those using predominantly electronic equipment. At the request of Department 1 a fleet commander will temporarily detach a naval or auxiliary vessel to carry out a reconnaissance mission. Merchant shipping is also liable to be used for reconnaissance, and on every ship the captain's first assistant is a Department 1 man. In some cases he is a naval officer, but more usually he is a merchant marine officer recruited for service with military intelligence. Standing in for the captain during the day – the captain is on duty at night – the first assistant observes all maritime activity in the neighbourhood of the ship and immediately reports sightings of foreign vessels to the department. Theoretically the captain is not a member of the intelligence service but, having formerly been a first assistant himself, he is fully aware of the situation. Indeed, on meeting a vessel at night he passes on this information via the first assistant, who has direct contact. A ship can be directed by military intelligence to cary out a special operation at any time. When this happens there is no need to explain to the captain, first assistant and radio operator what Department 1 is, what it does and what authority is has.

Department 2 is concerned with current agent intelligence. Officers are given special training (three years at the Military Diplomatic Academy) in the recruitment of foreign nationals; this is carried on in all Soviet ports, with particular emphasis on Swedes. In addition, any foreigners visiting the Soviet Union, including students, tourists, seamen, trade representatives, civilian pilots and stewardesses, are seen as potential agents. Though each military district, fleet and group of forces carries out this work independently, recruitment is also undertaken by the central organisation of the GRU. In turn, non-Soviet agents seek to recruit other people upon returning to their own countries.

Spetsnaz troopers training for close-quarter combat.

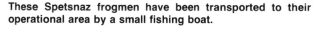

These Spetsnaz frogmen have been transported to their operational area by a small fishing boat.

The recruitment trawl also includes people within the Soviet Union and the Eastern Bloc countries who have relatives living abroad. Officers of the department rarely travel abroad themselves, contact with agents being effected either on Soviet territory or via couriers; other means include Soviet lorry drivers, foreign drivers recruited in the USSR, the postal and radio services.

Department 3 recruits independently of Department 2. While Department 2 agents are principally intended for the collection of information, Department 3 personnel are tasked with the sabotage, assassination and other special operations (*Spetsnaz*). Recruitment and communications are run on the same lines as in Department 2.

The whole system is characterised by extensive checks and balances. The commander of the RU can at any time run a check on a Department 2 operation using agents of Department 3, and vice versa. Similarly, the commander of Directorate 5 of the GRU can use Departments 2 or 3 of the Leningrad or Baltic military districts to check the operations being run by the commander of the Baltic Fleet RU.

Apart from Department 3 of its RU, the Baltic Fleet has a naval Spetsnaz brigade. This includes an anti-VIP company made up of professional sportsmen, a group of small submarines, two battalions of assault swimmers and one battalion of swimmer-parachutists. In the event of a conflict the anti-VIP company would attempt the elimination of Sweden's military and political leaders. Although the Leningrad and Baltic military district RUs are targetted against Sweden, it is the Baltic Fleet that is responsible for the elimination of Swedish VIPs. Danish and Finnish leaders are the concern of the Baltic and Leningrad military districts respectively. If the Swedish Government showed sufficient indecision in a crisis it would not be eliminated immediately, there being some advantage in keeping such a government in power. If this were to happen, then all the efforts of the anti-VIP company would be concentrated on the leaders of the armed forces and the police. The group of small submarines is intended for the transportation of Spetsnaz raiders and for carrying out special operations in enemy waters. The assault swimmers and swimmer/parachutist battalions are tasked with various diversionary activities both in the water and on land.

Department 4 processes the information gathered by the Baltic Fleet and the merchant vessels that ply the Baltic. The most important product is then passed on to GRU headquarters.

Department 5 is concerned with electronic intelligence. At its disposal it has ground-based electronic intelligence stations as well as ships and aircraft with special equipment. It is this department that controls the whole electronic intelligence network on naval and merchant vessels and military aircraft.

It can happen that a single Soviet merchant vessel carries officers from all five RU departments. Sometimes one officer will carry out his duties independently of the others, sometimes they all work together on the same mission. In the latter case, the group would be headed by a representative of the RU commander.

The weapons of aggression

The Soviet Union carried out some very interesting work on small submarines in the 1930s. The problem was put to several competing groups of designers at the same time, and in 1936 a government commission looked at the results: *Mosquito* (from the team led by B. M. Malinin), *Blokha* ("flea") (B. L. Byezhinski), and APSS and *Pigmy* (both from B. I. Bekauri). All four were transportable by small cargo or naval vessels. Development of the K-class (cruiser) submarine was completed at the same time. These boats could each carry a light aircraft or small submarine. Also investigated during this period was the possiblity of carrying an APSS small submarine aboard a TB-3 heavy bomber.

In 1939 B. L. Byezhinski produced the M-400 (Project 95) small submarine for the NKVD. This craft, a hybrid submarine-cum-motor torpedo boat (MTB), could run for long periods submerged before surfacing to attack its target at high speed with two torpedo tubes or a single 45mm gun. It could also make a high-speed approach before diving and attacking the target from close range. Its completion was halted in 1942 by German artillery fire. Also under development at this time was an engine that could be used in small submarines. Once again, a number of design teams were put to work on the same project. In 1938 the M-92

A proportion of all Spetsnaz troopers are trained parachutists.

Photograph and artist's impression of the German wartime small submarine known as *Delphin*. It is believed that the current Soviet type being used in the Baltic is an enlarged version of this design.

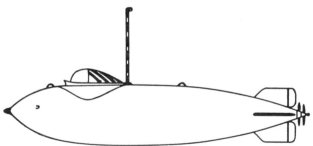

submarine was modernised by removing the batteries and replacing them with a single gas-fuelled engine designed by S. A. Basilevski. May 31, 1941, saw the launch of the M-401, powered by a single closed-cycle diesel engine designed by A. S. Kassatsir. This interesting work was interrupted by the war, resuming once more in 1945. During the war Soviet forces in the South-East Baltic had captured a German submarine research centre and with it a huge quantity of documents. The Soviet secret services hunted down the German designers, and their drawings were widely used in the construction of Soviet models. In some cases vessels were built directly to German plans. Other Soviet designs incorporated advances developed during the war by the Germans, among them navigation systems, recycling of air, and improved torpedo guidance.

Also captured were a number of complete small submarines and details of future projects, all of which were widely put to use by Soviet designers. This interest in German projects has persisted until the present. In 1976 information about wartime German plans to construct a submarine with a displacement of 90 tons came to light, whereupon the GRU immediately began tracking down the blueprints and the design team.

This evidence of interest in foreign armaments is not however indicative of technological backwardness in the Soviet Union, which has many talented design engineers who have created contemporary technological miracles. It is simply that the West uses its own ideas, while Soviet engineers use theirs plus others' too. In recent years some remarkable examples of weaponry have been developed in the Soviet Union, including small submarines for crews of one to five men. The Spetsnaz naval brigades have between them several dozen small submarines, and intensive efforts are being put into the development of hybrid craft capable of performing as both submarines and submarine-tractors.

Larger craft – naval ships, submarines and even fishing vessels – are used for transporting small submarines. In the 1960s tests were run in the Caspian Sea on a heavy glider (designed by O. K. Antonov) capable of ferrying a small submarine. The results are not known, but if such a glider were produced one could expect small submarines to appear during hostilities in the least likely locations – the Persian Gulf, for example

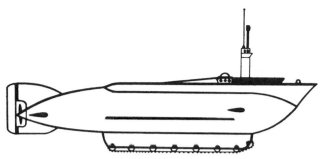

Artist's impression of the German *Seeteufel* or *Elefant* bottom-walking submarine. About 45ft long, this craft was designed to overcome the problems of launching conventional small submarines by paddling straight into the sea on its tracks. Although the prototype was destroyed at Lübeck there is little doubt that the Soviets obtained the plans for this and many other unconventional craft.

— even before the arrival of Soviet troops and larger vessels. In the 1960s and 1970s the Soviet Union also worked on the development of a miniature seaplane which could land on water and then dive to a depth of several metres.

Small submarines: how dangerous?

small submarines can be very dangerous, penetrating and operating in areas where normal submarines have no freedom of movement. It is possible to build several of these small submersibles for less than the cost of one medium-sized standard vessel, while for the enemy the destruction of a number of smaller craft poses a greater problem than that of one medium-sized submarine. A small submarine can also serve as a mobile base for assault swimmers, a combination which can be used successfully against both naval and land-based targets.

Small submarines and sabotage groups could be highly effective in both peace and war. After hostilities had begun, such teams could clear the way for the main body of the fleet by neutralising minefields, obstacles and hydro-acoustic devices. Many naval forces, particularly those of the Scandinavian countries, have developed strong, well protected shelters in which ships and submarines can be concealed with a high degree of security. These vessels would have to be dealt with quickly, in time of war, and the means used would probably be Spetsnaz teams. Military divers carried in small submarines could be used against bridges, docks, port installations and tunnels. Even more dangerous would be the use of Spetsnaz against underwater cables. It is likely that satellite communications and the conventional radio network would be severely disrupted by jamming and nuclear explosions in the atmosphere, with the result that Spetsnaz action against underground and marine cables would be very effective. In peacetime Spetsnaz could locate these cables and tap them for information, or, working with Osnaz signal-interception teams, use them to feed in false data. It is not out of the question that both Spetsnaz and Osnaz are currently operating in Swedish waters.

But the greatest danger of submarine operations in the territorial waters of a sovereign and neutral state is political rather than military. The most desirable object in war is to force the enemy to give up without a fight. Many aggressors have used their strength as a political weapon, forcing their opponents to capitulate without firing a shot. This is how Hitler played his cards in the case of Austria and Czechoslovakia, how Stalin dealt with Estonia, Lithuania and Latvia, how the Soviet Union is now working on Sweden. A war of nerves can go on for a long time, but the Soviet leaders are in no hurry. Has the West enough resolve to support Sweden? Has the Swedish Government enough resolve to defend its country? Does it have the courage to destroy an intruding vessel at the right moment? Let us hope that it has.

How good is Soviet naval manpower?

Capt John Moore RN and Theodor Ghoshal

In 1801 George Canning, addressing the British House of Commons, made a statement which naval planners would do well to recall in these days of galloping technology: "If the distinction must be taken, men are everything, measures comparatively nothing." As politicians add up meaningless lists of tonnages, designers are seduced by the spectacle of the latest shiny device, and naval staffs compute the amount of fuel a new gas turbine will guzzle, there is a growing tendency to forget the importance of "the man" and, to a growing extent, "the woman" in a navy. Time and again journalists want to know which navy is No 1, having failed to appreciate the wide range of factors which must be considered when evaluating a single fleet, let alone comparing one with another. Of these factors, the most important is the condition of those who man the ships. This is a function of their background, training, experience, morale, discipline,

length of service and leadership, to mention only some of the terms in this most complex of equations.

There is therefore no sense in considering the effectiveness of the Soviet Navy without having some knowledge of its people. First, its huge manpower total of half a million – including 350,000 conscripts must be analysed as to activity and rank. The fleets and squadrons absorb 200,000 men, naval aviation 68,000, naval infantry 15,000, coastal defence 14,000, training 57,000 and shore support 146,000. Roughly 20% of them are officers, 10% warrant officers and extended servicemen, and 70% conscripts serving three years

---

Heading picture Soviet Navy anti-aircraft gun crew pictured during an exercise. How well would these men work together in the heat of combat? (*Novosti*)

afloat or two years ashore. Women may also volunteer but, in contrast with the merchant navy, they all serve ashore.

Bottom of the pyramid but essential to the running of the navy are the conscripts. The Soviet serviceman or woman has been brought up from infancy to revere the name of Lenin, the doctrine of Marxist-Leninism and the state. As time passes, service with the Pioneers, the Komsomol (Young Communists' League) and the junior military training organisation, DOSAAF, continues this indoctrination. Thus, by the time the young man of 18 is conscripted, he has had little chance to consider any other viewpoint. He now starts six months' training and two and a half years' service in a ship, during which a third of his waking hours will be spent in the care of the political officer. It is at this time that he is taught the need for an idealistic approach, devotion and dilligence in his labours, and a hatred for his country's enemies. This might be numbing stuff for some but could be an inspiration for others at a formative period of their lives.

Once in the service, the conscript will be taught and commanded in Russian, a trial for the growing number whose native language is one of the more than 100 tongues spoken in the USSR. He is supposed to speak Russian as taught at school, but across the 22.5 million square kilometres of the USSR (two and a half times the size of the USA) the main thrust of teaching is in the

towns, leaving widely spread rural millions to slip through the instructional net. This deficiency was remedied in Imperial days by taking the conscripts from Russian-speaking areas, but now the immense size of the armed forces make it necessary to wield the conscript scoop throughout the vast federation. The problem is made worse by the fact that the distribution of the Soviet population is changing. In 1970 59 per cent of the population spoke Russian as their mother tongue. Today, with the inadequate accommodation of the western cities and towns restricting many people to one-child families, the demographic balance is shifting steadily to the east.

Language difficulties apart, this also results in interracial friction. A Kazakh from Alma-Ata would find it as hard to have instant rapport with an Estonian from Tallin as would an Indian from Paraguay with an inhabitant of Jamaica. Such differences not infrequently lead to violence, another reason for the castiron discipline imposed in the Soviet forces.

Basic seamanship training at the Novorossiysk Marine School. Though destined to serve in the merchant fleet, these sailors wear naval-style uniforms, row naval ship's boats, and could in emergency be called on to perform naval tasks. (*Novosti*)

The seagoing part of the navy has numerous advantages for the authorities over the shore element, the army and the air and rocket forces. There is less chance of the all-pervading drunkenness of the Soviet citizenry affecting a ship's company, cooped up as they are. There is less opportunity for desertion and there is greater scope for surveillance by the ship's officers. What spare time the sailors have is spent mainly on board, with the result that the incidence of theft and vandalism is lower than amongst land-bound youths.

Once the conscript's shore training is completed – here it should be emphasised that the figure 57,000 given above represents only half the total trained each year – he joins his ship for on-the-job instruction under the guidance of his predecessor. The latter is released once the new boy has satisfied his officers of his competence, and he is subsequently granted third-class specialist rate. If he is diligent at his work and studies he can reach first-class rate in a year at the age of 19½. Such speed of advancement would cause apoplexy in many senior rates' messes in Western navies.

He soon becomes involved in the apparently endless round of standardised competitions between vessels of the same squadron, class or type. Performance in these tests, plus points for the number of specialists and outstanding ratings on board, is used in calculating the

Naval infantrymen disembark from BTR-60P amphibious armoured personnel carriers, with Polnochny-class LSMs in the background. (*Novosti*)

Morning exercises to the strains of the ship's band aboard a *Sverdlov*-class cruiser. (*Novosti*)

ship's standing in the navy. Anybody who recalls the desperate artifices employed before an admiral's inspection – the rush to produce a full muster of "qualified swimmers," the dolts transferred to the sick bay – will understand how this far more rigorous system must promote all kinds of abuses.

If the conscript expects all this effort, devotion, diligence and idealism to yield him any financial reward, he's in for a nasty shock on his first visit to the pay table. His basic pay is about £3 per month, with an extra 80p when he is in an operational ship. Additional allowances of £2 and £4 per month go with 2nd and 1st-class specialist rates respectively. There is however no extra pay for higher substantive rating up to Petty Officer 1st Class. More pay can be allowed for positions of particular responsibility, such as team leader on a gun or sonar set, but the total monthly pay of a conscript with the highest qualifications will never exceed about £20. The above "abouts" are due to the fluctuating value of sterling and the endless arguments over the

value of the rouble, but the fact remains that the junior conscript can barely keep himself in writing paper. We shall see later how this compares, in a socialist society, with the "emoluments" of an officer.

The living conditions of the junior sailors are reminiscent of those prevailing in the Royal Navy 50 years ago: cramped and uncomfortable. The food is dull by Western standards, although both lodgings and rations are probably no worse than many men are accustomed to at home. In these surroundings the Soviet conscript spends two and a half years under stern discipline and endless indoctrination. He may operate only one item of equipment, or at most two if he is bright and cross-trained. Physically tough and generally imbued with a sense of duty and patriotism, he would in the event of war probably show himself as courageous and long-suffering as his father was during the Great Patriotic War. But his knowledge of technical matters is necessarily sketchy and there must be some doubt about his ability to cope with crises such as battle damage. Initiative is not his forte.

Those who choose to re-enlist are taken on for further spells of two, four or six years. A number of these chief petty officers are taken on as warrant officers and, eventually, senior warrant officers. Translation to

Ratings and an accordion-playing petty officer take a musical break in the shadow of a Kresta II-class cruiser. Note the difference in the quality of the two types of uniform. (*Novosti*)

officer status from this position is possible, but it is in this vital area between the mess deck and the wardroom that the main problems of manning have arisen. The warrant officer starts at a rate of £135 a month and is eligible for 30 days' leave each year, which compares very favourably with the conscript's ration of zero in his first year and, if he is lucky, ten days in each of his second and third years.

The training of officers is designed to overcome the lack of technical ability in those who will be in their charge. Once a candidate has passed the selection board he is entered as a cadet and undergoes five years' training (four years for political officers). If he is good enough he will then receive an engineering diploma and the rank of lieutenant. Only the best are sent to sea, since just 40% of the total strength serves in ships.

Each officer's speciality has by this time been decided for him and he will stay in the same ship for many years, sometimes emerging in command. Absurd at first sight, this scheme makes more sense when it is realised that the officers are the only people on board with a thorough technical training. They are responsible not only for supervising their sailors' duties and political upbringing but also for carrying out all but the most elementary maintenance tasks. One result of this, referred to regularly in Soviet writings, is an inability to accept the need for deligation of responsibility.

Ship's boat from a SAM Kotlin-class destroyer photographed from a US Navy carrier during a Soviet exercise in the Mediterranean. The matelots seem cheerful enough, but only the petty officers wear lifejackets. (*US Navy*)

As the officer progresses in seniority so his experience broadens until he is considered fit for command. Once in this position he must pass additional examinations before being allowed to take his ship to sea independently. By this time he will probably find that his officers are far more numerous than would be the case in a similar ship in a Western navy. There might be 25 or more officers in an elderly Kashin-class destroyer and many more in a ballistic missile submarine, while in an Alfa-class submarine all the ship's company of 40 are with very few exceptions officers or senior ratings.

During his first command a Soviet naval officer will also often undertake a postgraduate course, to be followed by a two-year course in Leningrad. After further staff and command experience the "high-flyer" will go to Moscow for another lengthy course, this time a joint gathering at the Academy of the General Staff. From this fount of all knowledge he will emerge as a candidate for flag rank, every effort having been made to broaden his views from the narrow specialist approach which was his for the first 15 years or so in the profession. These constrictions of experience, allied with an inherent concern to act in a manner acceptable to his immediate superiors, probably produce an officer less inclined than his Western counterpart to act with balance and initiative.

Soviet naval personnel of every rank have to attend comulsory courses in communist ideaology, propaganda and policy. On board Soviet warships political education serves the party's purpose of maintaining tight control and discipline throughout the navy. Every Soviet warship has its CO and political Number One, who are both responsible to the party for the organisa-

tion of political education. The curriculum comprises Marxist-Leninist traiing of officers, political education of chief petty officers, political classes for sailors and leading seamen, education in the spirit of the party, and cultural activities, including discussion of the "aesthetic" nature of military activity. Officers are thereby conditioned to toe the party line, being forced to recognise the infallibility of Marx and Lenin as currently interpreted by the Polituro. CPOs are indoctrinated in similar fashion, and in turn brainwash ratings so that they become the willing tools of their immediate superiors.

During a voyage not a day passes without party policy being aired to the whole ship's company. All policy decisions are backed up by ideological reasoning. To boost fighting morale even more, the individual sailor is encouraged to exteriorise any frustrations he may have in the form of hatred for a vaguely defined "class enemy".

To round off this consideration of the personnel of the world's largest socialist navy, there is the matter of rewards. As in the navy of the tsars, compared with his men the officer lives in conditions of the greatest comfort. His base pay is a combination of rank and position pay. This can be trebled to account for the area and conditions of his service if he is likely to be involved in conflict, while doubling is frequent in peacetime. Other additions are annual increments (15% after ten years and then 1% per year), sea pay and specialist pay (e.g. submarines and Spetsnaz). The whole pay code is so complex that it is impossible for anyone but a Soviet paymaster to offer any concrete examples. Suffice it to say that while a Western flag officer may receive four or five times the pay of an able seaman, his Soviet opposite number's factor of increase will be in the hundreds.

Artist's depiction of Soviet sailors in close combat at Sevastopol in 1942. Though few doubt the potentially heroic qualities of today's Russian naval personnel, do they have enough flexibility and technical expertise to prevail in modern warfare?

It is very difficult to form conclusions on the likely performance of the people of the Soviet Navy under battle conditions. They would undoubtedly be brave and tenacious. But would the fabric hold together under conditions of action damage? Would the officers show the initiative needed to turn a difficult situation to their advantage? The outcome to any future naval engagement would depend on the answers to these two questions, and I personally feel that in each case Soviet officers and men might be found wanting.

Soviet submarines: new cruise missiles compound the problem

Capt John Moore RN

It has been customary over the last 25 years to divide the Soviet submarine force into three distinct groups: the strategic missile, the cruise missile and the attack submarines. Now new missile developments have blurred the divisions between these categories. The arrival of the SS-NX-21 tube-launched cruise missile, with a range greater than that of some ballistic missiles, means that SSNs so fitted are now capable of strategic land bombardment, resulting in a great increase in total capability. The larger follow-on weapon will give a further improvement, though both systems will require careful integration into the targeting plan of the Strategic Rocket Forces. The entire concept bristles with potential problems of command and control, but from now on the NATO navies must regard a whole new group of boats as both attack submarines and long-range cruise missile platforms.

Erosion of the distinction between cruise missile and attack submarines first began about ten years ago. Introduction of the SS-N-15, armed with a nuclear head and capable of being launched from the torpedo tubes of the Victors and Alfas, enlarged the attack range of these boats to 50nm+. Admittedly this weapon – and the longer-range SS-N-16 – has a ballistic trajectory, but this merely compounds the problem.

A salvo of SS-N-16s armed with torpedoes or nuclear depth bombs fired from a Victor-class SSN would go a long way towards thwarting the plans of a battle-group commander.

Given the complications outlined above, it is probably best to consider the changes in the Soviet submarine fleet in chronological order.

Class	First commissioned
Kilo	1981
Oscar	1981
Typhoon	1983
Sierra	1983
Mike	1984

Heading picture Though the appearance of the Mike class came as no great surprise to Western observers, their great size was unexpected. Displacing nearly 4,000 tons more than the 6,000-ton Victor IIIs, Mike is also significantly faster. It is therefore now believed that the class is not an upgraded Victor III but an expansion of the Alfa class, with a titanium hull and liquid metal-cooled reactor.

The Victor III class incorporated improved silencing, the last stage in the improvement of conventional nuclear-propelled submarines, following increased speed, greater weapon load and deeper diving. The 31ft-long stern pod is generally regarded as a base for a towed array. It could in fact be an effective fixed array, located as it is well above hull and screw noise.

The Kilo class has been built at Komsomolsk at the rate of one a year since the first was completed there in 1981. This is the first operational diesel-electric submarine type to be built by the USSR, although the larger rescue submarines of the India class (first commissioned in 1978) probably also use this form of propulsion. A further variation compared with the preceding Tango class is the reduction of the beam/length ratio to 1:7.36 from the 1:10.15 of the latter. The resulting rather chubby submarine has a length of 239.5ft and a dived displacement of 3,000 tons. Though large by Western standards, this is 1,000 tons less than the Tangos and has allowed an increase of about 1.5kt to 17kt dived speed despite a reduction in the total horsepower on a single shaft. Part of the Kilo

Victor III in heavy weather. The gouts of water from the limber holes (normally capped when dived) show that the problem of hull-induced noise has not yet been overcome.

size reduction results from the omission of the four stern tubes fitted to the Tango and Foxtrot boats. Photographs show no sign of a fore-hatch, suggesting that torpedoes are loaded via the bow tubes with the boat trimmed by the stern, as practised by the Federal German Navy.

The purpose of this additional new design is unclear, but it is probably nothing more complex than a response to the need for a replacement for the ageing Whiskey and Romeo classes. If this is the case, an acceleration in building rate is to be expected in the near future. With their *Albacore*-style single-screw hull, anechoic covering and, presumably, modern sound-damping, the Kilos despite their size are useful boats for operations within the continental shelf.

As details of the single Papa-class boat emerged after her commissioning in 1971 it became obvious that the Soviets had produced something very different from the Charlie I-class SSGN. A twin-screw boat with a new hull form, she had ten instead of eight inclined missile tubes and a distinctive surface profile. The fact that only one Papa was built made it likely that she was the experimental forerunner of a larger and more heavily armed new class.

The first of these Oscar boats, commissioned in 1981, strongly resembles Papa but, as expected, is much larger. The outer hull contains not only the large pressure hull but also six twin SS-N-19 launch tubes on each side, running from just abaft the fin to a position some 20ft abaft the retractable foreplanes. This

arrangement means that there is a cushion of water some 11–12ft thick between the two hulls, forming a useful protection against the explosion of a torpedo at the outer skin.

The twin shafts are similar to those in Papa, although the Oscars' 14,000 tons dived displacement will almost certainly have called for an increase in horsepower if the earlier boat's 35kt maximum speed is to be maintained. There is a strong possibility that the very large casing contains both a communications buoy and a towed-array sonar. As in other modern Soviet submarines, the secondary armament of torpedoes may well include the 24½in weapons, whose range, if the Japanese Type 93 Long Lance of 50 years ago is any guide, might be as great as 30–35 miles. This submarine is capable of attacking a battle group, without surfacing, from a range out to the 300-mile limit of the SS-N-19 cruise missiles. These are probably sea-skimmers in the closing part of their flight but may have no more penetration capability with HE heads than their Western counterparts. What is certain, however, is that when fitted with nuclear heads the 24 missiles carried would be capable of disrupting a major naval force.

In September 1980 the first of the long-expected Typhoon class was launched. ("Typhoon" is the accepted NATO term: variations such as "Taifun" are unofficial.) This giant, with a dived displacement of at least 29–30,000 tons and dimensions of 557ft × 75ft, is the largest submarine type ever conceived. Design work must have started in the late 1960s or early 1970s, at which time the concept represented an enormous advance on the first true SSBNs, the Yankee class, which began to enter service in 1967. It also represented part of a huge drawing office load for the submarine programme alone at that time, when five completely new designs and many modifications to existing classes were under way simultaneously.

Typhoon is completely different from any previous

Oscar appears to be the ultimate design of nuclear-propelled specialist cruise missile submarine. Displacing 14,000 tons dived and with a maximum underwater speed of about 35kt, she carries 24 SS-N-19s in inclined tubes. These missiles have a range of 350nm and can be targeted with satellite information; this avoids the need for a vulnerable third-party ship or aircraft.

|←———————————— 560 ft ————————————→|

The designers responsible for Typhoon must have faced for-midable control problems. With its huge length of 557.6ft, dived displacement nearing 30,000 tons and dived speed of at least 30kt (probably a great deal more), this "boat" is prob-ably controlled by computers capable of reacting instantly to any variation of trim or angle. Visible in this drawing are features suggesting that Typhoon was designed for under-ice operations: the massive casing, the double-stepped fin and the location of the foreplanes forward instead of on the fin.

SSBN design, having a huge outer casing containing the main body of the submarine. The 20 launch tubes for the SS-NX-20 missiles are located forward of the large fin, which has a complex profile incorporating sloping sections, both forward and aft, designed to minimise drag. A further move in the direction is the mounting of the foreplanes in the bow rather than on the fin.

Several things make it probable that this class was designed for under-ice operations: the twin-level fin; the heavily curved, massive casing, with its high freeboard; and the location of the foreplanes on the fore-casing rather than the fin. The large fin has the usual masts and there is clearly room for at least one VLF, or even ELF, communications buoy. If under-ice operations are to be an important part of the duties of this class, it would be prudent to fit two such buoys. A towed-array sonar is also likely to be fitted.

The solid-propellant SS-NX-20 has a range of some 5,500 miles and is fitted with at least six MIRVs. Curi-ously, only 20 missiles are carried. The torpedo arma-ment is probably similar to that of other new designs, comprising a total of six 21in and 24½in tubes in the bow, with three reloads per tube. It is likely that some of these torpedoes can be replaced by either SS-N-15 missiles carrying a depth bomb or SS-N-16s with a depth bomb or a homing torpedo; both can be launched from a normal 21in torpedo tube. No other weapon systems have been identified so far, but it would come

The Sierra class is a logical follow-on from Victor III of about 8,500 tons dived displacement. With slightly more speed than the later Victors, these boats were expected to form the Victor IV class. The pod on the after stabiliser differs in shape from the Victor III installation, but the purpose is certainly the same: long-range sonar operations.

as no surprise if the Typhoons turned out to be fitted with submarine-to-air missiles similar to the Vickers SLAM, which completed trials 12 years ago. Equally likely is a specialised air-warning radar. After all, Allied submarines were fitted with simple air-search radars 40 years ago, and the threat is far greater today. The extraordinary value of submarines of this class would justify the use of every form of sensor and weapon installation.

There was a short pause after the arrival of Typhoon before the first of the two anticipated SSN classes was observed. This was Mike, a very large submarine of nigh on 10,000 tons dived which may well continue the programme of titanium pressure hulls begun with the Alfa and Papa classes. Built at Severodvinsk at the same yard as Papa, Mike is a 400ft-long single-screw submarine armed with 21in and 24½in torpedoes and SS-NX-21 1,600nm-range shore-bombardment cruise missiles, all probably tube-launched. If the hull is made of titanium alloys, and bearing in mind the Soviet Navy's long experience with this type of hull construction, the diving depth for Mike may well be in excess of the 2,500ft estimated for Alfa. Continuing the comparison with Alfa, which has for some time been

regarded as a test class for a future design, there is a reasonable chance that the 40ft of beam makes room for twin liquid-metal-cooled reactors of a larger capacity than that fitted to Alfa. Despite this, the much larger hull means that maximum speed is probably in the 35kt+ range, compared with Alfa's 42kt. Nonetheless, there is no doubt that Mike is a very formidable war vessel.

Until more is known of the Sierra class, the next to come off the slips, Western analysts can only continue to guess as to the need for yet another design. Initial information on the first of class, which was built at Gorky, suggests that this may be a further extension of the original Victor design, stretched in the beam rather than in length. The resultant increase in displacement to something over 8,000 tons dived might have been expected to result in a loss of speed, but it seems likely that the overall horsepower has been increased to give something comfortably over 30kt. With an armament similar to that of Mike, Sierra's steel pressure hull and PW reactor probably make it the Soviet Union's "cheap" SSN design, to be produced in greater numbers than the very expensive Mikes.

The difference between Soviet methods of ship procurement and those of Western navies is exemplified by this variety of new classes. The US Navy, with the *Ohio* and *Los Angeles* classes in production, is tinkering with the idea of a new class of SSNs. In the UK there is much agonising over the cost of the Trident SLBM; there is no news of a successor to the *Trafalgar* class; and the Type 2400 SS looks like being too large and costly for the Royal Navy's requirements. By contrast, the Soviet Navy has in the last five years produced four types of huge underwater warship in the Typhoon, Oscar, Mike and Sierra classes, as well as Kilo, the non-operational though important India, Lima and Uniform, and an as

The first Alfa-class boat was launched at Sudomekh Yard, Leningrad, in 1969. The hull remained alongside being fitted out for the best part of two years, and then suffered some form of disaster. In 1974 the submarine was scrapped. Two years later the second Alfa appeared, to be followed by five more. Initial assessments that these titanium-hulled boats with liquid metal-cooled reactors were test vehicles with an operational capability were confirmed when the first of the Mike class appeared. Even so, a 3,800-ton submarine which can run at 42kt and dive to at least 2,500ft, and which requires a crew of only 40–45 people, is clearly a great advance.

Alfa, the fastest submarine in the world.

yet undesignated nuclear-powered research submarine. Add to this the modifications to the Yankee, Hotel, Golf and Echo II classes, and it becomes plain that a continuing programme of addition and adaptation is proceeding at an accelerating rate.

There is very clear evidence of unrelenting investigation and development of a wide spectrum of improvements in submarine design. These currently cover basic hull design, the shaping of the fin, what the Soviets term "unsinkability," the extensive use of titanium alloys in both hull and internal construction, the reduction of drag by numerous means such as the use of "compliant" coverings and the secretion of polymers from this outer skin, the reduction of magnetic signatures, and the use of automatic control systems. By 1984 a number of other advances were clearly in train, covering propulion, boundary-layer control, the use of unconventional materials and the reduction of the various signatures by which a submarine may be located. Specific developments are believed to include super-conducting electrical machinery, magneto hydrodynamic generators which pass a conductive plasma through a magnetic field and can be used as a form of submerged jet engine, thermo-electric generators, fuel cells and gas-cooled reactors similar to the US Nerva project, which, though successful, was dropped in 1973. Evidence suggests that at least the first two of this list are already at sea.

Faced with this array of technological advances, which are aimed at improving a submarine's advantages and decreasing its disadvantages, those charged with planning Western anti-submarine warfare have a formidable task. Continuity of thought, innovation and originality, flexibility of approach and the discarding of the belief that "the Soviets are thinkers, not doers" are essential and long overdue.

Gorshkov, architect of the balanced fleet

Capt John Moore RN

Recently there have been certain small-minded mutterings in the West concerning the part played by Admiral of the Fleet of the Soviet Union Sergei Gorshkov in combining many diverse types of ship into what looks like becoming in the next 15 years the most powerful and best balanced fleet in the world's history. But no professional could deny that this man has achieved more in the 28 years since he assumed supreme power in the Soviet Navy than any other single sailor, group or collection of committees has done in any other fleet. It is therefore prudent to pay attention to what Admiral Gorshkov has to say about the operation of surface fleets.

The following quotations from *Sea Power of the State* (Pergamon Press) reflect the thinking of a man who was for many years a highly professional and successful naval officer whose political preoccupations came only in later years.

- "Surface ships remain the basic and often sole com-

Heading picture Frunze **with the helicopter hangar open and showing the new twin 130mm turret which replaced the two single 100mm guns in** *Kirov.* **(***RAF***)**

bat means of ensuring deployment of the main strike forces of the fleet, submarines." (page 196)

● "Surface ships form the basis of the land disembarking aids and forces of support for a landing. They have the chief role in the fight against the mine danger and in protecting communications." (page 197)

● "In closed theatres and in coastal areas surface ships may be employed for operations on sea communications." (page 197)

● "As shown by the conflicts of the post-war period, surface ships are capable of solving a large range of tasks in local wars." (page 197)

● "The development and building of surface ships are in keeping with their potential in the creation of a modern balanced nuclear missile fleet. Numerically the largest group is made up of anti-submarine surface ships." (page 197)

There follows a piece on the efficacy of missile-armed ships and craft against the surface and merchant ships of the enemy. Then Gorshkov moves to the need to "rebuff successfully air attacks from the enemy." Concluding this section, he writes of the need for special-ised amphibious vessels: "Only in the second post-war decade did the fleet receive specially built landing craft."

Having allocated slightly more than a page to conventional surface ships, Gorshkov gives almost two pages to the naval applications of air-cushion, hydrofoil and wing-in-ground-effect (WIG) craft, and a further two to naval air. He believes that "helicopters are a constituent part of modern surface ships" (page 200), and completes this part of his thesis with the statement: "The combat possibilities of naval aviation are one of the salient indicators of the strike power of our modern

Artist's impression of the Soviet nuclear-propelled aircraft carrier now under construction at Nikolayev. Of about 75,000 tons, she will probably carry 75 aircraft and will be the first fixed-wing carrier ever completed for the Soviet Navy. Points of interest in this drawing are the vertical-launch systems for missiles, the angled deck and the fixed radar arrays on the island.

navy. Naval aviation has in fact become oceanic, it has been converted into a most important means of armed struggle at sea." (page 202)

At this stage readers may wonder where they are being led. The answer is simple: to an understanding of the Soviet Navy's inexorable march towards the "balanced fleet," the objective which Admiral Gorshkov has sought throughout his long period in office. Admiral Gorshkov requires the following capabilities in such a fleet:

- Escort of submarines (with naval air forces, the most important elements of the fleet)
- Anti-surface ship operations
- Amphibious assault
- Mine countermeasures
- Interdiction of seaborne communications
- Effective anti-submarine operations
- Defence against attacks by aircraft or missiles
- The use of both fixed and rotary-wing aircraft
- The employment of all forms of unconventional ships and craft

The Admiral may now be 74 years old but it is obvious that he and his subordinates have a clear vision of the future shape and size of their fleet. How does the current building programme fit into this pattern?

Although the wording in *Sea Power of the State* suggests only the escort of submarines deploying into the open oceans, there is also a need to protect ballistic missile submarines within the local and home waters of the USSR. Vital to the execution of these tasks is intelligence of NATO deployments. This can come from a number of sources: agents within NATO, mer-

chant or fishing fleets and intelligence ships (AGIs), satellites, submarines, intelligence buoys and aircraft. Some of these sources, such as the AGIs and satellites, may be short-lived, while the geographical situation of the USSR gives little scope for the use of underwater surveillance systems. The Northern Fleet command therefore faces a major intelligence problem which will only be eased by the arrival of fixed-wing, high-performance reconnaissance aircraft operating from the carrier currently under construction at Nikolayev.

Anti-surface ship operations would have a number of objectives: restriction of NATO anti-submarine operations, anti-carrier operations, reconnaissance of and attacks on NATO amphibious forces, and protection of

---

Frunze is the second of the *Kirov* class of battle-cruisers. These 25,000-ton ships, the third of which is building, are of a most unusual design, with both nuclear and conventional boiler power. Their formidable armament centres on 20 SS-N-19 SSMs (270nm range) housed in tubes set at 45° forward of the bridge. Forward of these are 12 SA-N-6 launch tubes with eight reloads apiece. In *Kirov* the bow position is occupied by a twin reloadable SS-N-14 anti-submarine missile launcher, the first in the Soviet Navy with this capability. In *Frunze* this has been replaced by a second SAM system, the vertical tubes of which are also located, four to port and starboard, beside the flight deck. Completed by two main-battery guns, eight Gatlings, two quadruple 21in torpedo tubes, an RBU 6000 anti-submarine rocket launcher and three helicopters in each ship, the all-round firepower of this class, backed by an impressive radar and ECM/ESM fit, is probably unmatched by any Western vessel short of a fleet carrier. (*RAF*)

Slava is the first of a class of four 12,000-ton (full load) cruisers built at Nikolayev. She was completed in mid-1982 and sailed from the Black Sea after trials in September 1983. This class carries 16 SS-N-12 SSMs (as in the *Kiev* class), eight vertical launchers for SA-N-6 missiles (64 carried), one of the new twin 130mm gun turrets, six Gatlings, two RBU 6000 anti-submarine rocket launchers, ten 21in torpedo tubes and a helicopter. Primary role of this class is surface action. (*Royal Navy*)

Slava, showing the Top Steer 3D air-search radar on the foremast and the Top Pair 3D early-warning radar just forward of the funnel. The Kite Screech radar above the bridge controls the 130mm guns, while the four Side Globe housings below Top Pair are for electronic warfare. The horned aerial below Top Steer is for the Front Door/Front Piece radar, which provides tracking for the SS-N-12 missiles. (*US Navy*)

Soviet own amphibious operations. These last might be aimed at the NATO islands of Svalbard, Jan Mayen, Iceland and the Faeroes, as well as the Norwegian coast.

A factor which always affects operations in the vicinity of the Arctic Circle, which skims the north coast of Iceland and passes just south of Bodø in northern Norway, is the ferocity of the weather. The Admiralty Pilot remarks that "with the exception of the region off north-east Greenland, most of the sea area under discussion is exceptionally wild and stormy." These conditions also exist in the operating area of the other major Soviet fleet, based at Vladivostok and Petropavlovsk and operating in the Pacific. If ships are to operate for long periods under these conditions, they must be designed for extended range and an increased ability

Sovremenny, first ship of a class of at least eight surface warfare destroyers, was commissioned in 1980. Displacing 7,800 tons full load, they have a maximum speed of 34kt and carry eight SS-N-22 missiles (an improved SS-N-9 with a range of about 120nm). A single Helix helicopter is carried for over-the-horizon targeting; the Bandstand radar in the dome above the bridge serves for line-of-sight firings. The class's designations − NATO "guided missile destroyer" and Soviet "eskadrenny minonosets", or destroyer − are equally illogical. Their hull and propulsion are the same as those of the Kresta I and II classes and their armament is more formidable, yet the Krestas are designated as cruisers by both authorities. (*Royal Navy*)

Udaloy, first of a class of at least eight ships, was commissioned in November 1980. Unlike the slightly smaller *Sovremenny*s, these ships are designated "large anti-submarine ships" by the Soviet Navy. This term is also applied to the Kara class, which, confusingly, are regarded as "guided missile cruisers" by NATO. Propulsion is by four gas turbines as opposed to the *Sovremenny*'s steam turbines, and armament comprises two Helix helicopters, eight SS-N-14 anti-submarine missiles, eight 21in torpedo tubes, two single 100mm guns and two RBU 6000 anti-submarine rocket launchers. A new form of vertical-launch SAM system is also installed. (*RAF*)

to ride very heavy seas. Such ships need not necessarily be large if the hull form is adequate. But the Soviets appear to have decided that they will continue to enlarge their designs, a result possibly of hard experience of the northern oceans. The four recent surface ship designs, the 28,000-ton *Kirov* class, the 13,000-ton *Slava*-class cruisers, and the destroyers of the *Sovremenny* and *Udaloy* classes, are all notably larger for their type than any since the *Sverdlov*-class cruisers of the 1950s.

This increase in size makes available extra firepower and electronics. *Kirov* has 20 inclined tubes for the long-range SS-N-19 cruise missiles, is the first ship to have SS-N-14 anti-submarine missile reloads, has eight reload salvoes for the twelve SA-N-6 SAM launchers, and carries a normal load of SA-N-4 SAMs. Also fitted are some three dozen fitments for ECM, ESM and IFF, and 19 radars varying from the Top Pair and Top Steer early-warning sets to the Fly Screen aircraft landing system. Completing this formidable weapon system fit are two 100mm guns and eight Gatlings. Variations have been shipped in the second of the class, *Frunze*. SS-N-14 has been displaced by a second vertical-launch SAM system, located further aft by the flight deck; the single guns have been replaced by a twin 130mm turret; and the after Gatlings have been moved up a deck. The result is a ship with a greatly improved AA capability at the expense of her long-range anti-submarine capability.

The *Slava* class, at 13,000 tons full load the modern equivalent of earlier cruisers, has an almost equally impressive armament. Sixteen long-range SS-N-12 missiles and a twin 130mm turret comprise the surface-to-surface armament. Eight SA-N-6 launchers with a total of 64 missiles, two twin SA-N-4 launchers, a new PDMS and six Gatlings provide for AA defence,

while underwater weapons comprise eight 21in torpedo tubes, two RBU 6000 rocket launchers, and either anti-submarine torpedoes or depth bombs delivered by the single Hormone or Helix helicopter.

These details are important to anyone seeking a pattern in the surface shipbuilding programmes. While *Kirov* has dual capability, *Frunze* is primarily orientated towards surface action in an area of air and missile threat. Both have very significant detection capabilities above, on and under the water, as well as advanced command and control facilities. *Slava* is designed for surface action, as is *Sovremenny*, while *Udaloy* is primarily an anti-submarine ship with a fair measure of self-protection.

Over the next two years the Soviet Navy will have acquired an ASW force of four *Kiev*-class VTOL/ helicopter carriers (also offering surface and intervention capability), seven Kara-class cruisers, ten Kresta II-class cruisers, the two *Moskva* helicopter carriers, eight *Udaloy*-class destroyers and 32 frigates of the

---

Novorossiysk is the third of four *Kiev*-class carriers capable of operating VTOL and rotary-wing aircraft. Displacing 43,000 tons full load and capable of 32kt, these heavily armed ships have a range of 13,500 miles at 18kt and 4,000 at 31kt. They carry a remarkable armament of eight SS-N-12 SSMs with 16 reloads, two twin SA-N-3 SAM launchers, four 76mm guns, eight 30mm Gatlings, a twin SUW-N-1 anti-submarine mounting and ten 21in torpedo tubes. The first pair, *Kiev* and *Minsk*, have SA-N-4 point-defence missile system mountings but in *Novorossiysk* these have been removed, probably to be replaced with a vertical-launch SAM system similar to that carried in the *Udaloy* class. Underwater sensors comprise a low-frequency hull-mounted sonar and a medium-frequency variable-depth sonar.

Krivak classes. Surface operations would require the four cruisers of the elderly Kynda-class, four Kresta I cruisers, three *Slava*-class, and seven *Sovremenny*-class. The older destroyers would be available as escorts for either type of force. Admiral Gorshkov has therefore achieved one of his aims, namely the biasing of his strength towards anti-submarine operations.

It is clear that the argument over the need for organic air support was decided some time ago in favour of the fixed-wing aircraft carrier. Gorshkov's comment that "naval aviation has become oceanic" can now be seen in its true perspective as the first Soviet nuclear carrier rapidly takes shape on the slips at Nikolayev. However, although she may be completed within the next two years, preparing her for sea, the trials and then the long process of learning the extremely difficult task of operating a carrier air wing will occupy a further lengthy period. Thus the first of these 75,000-ton ships is unlikely to be fully operational before 1992–3.

Grozyashchy is a Krivak II-class frigate, 11 of which were built at Kaliningrad. With the 21 ships of the Krivak I class and the single Krivak III, which appeared in October 1984, they are classified as "escort ships" by the Soviet Navy. The variations between I and II are comparatively minor. All carry four SS-N-14 anti-submarine missiles and two SA-N-4 SAM launchers. In Krivak I there are two twin 76mm gun mountings, replaced by a single twin 100mm mounting in Krivak II. The latter has a slightly larger VDS than the earlier ships, while the main difference in Krivak III is the addition of a helicopter.

Gorshkov's views on amphibious ships have resulted in a dual shipbuilding programme. Its naval element has created the two *Rogov*s, the Ropucha, Alligator and Polnochny classes, the minor landing craft, and the very large number of hovercraft and wing-in-ground-effect vehicles either in service or under construction. The building of major vessels, apart from one new design, has dropped off almost completely, leading some to assume that the requirement has largely been met. If it has, this must be thanks to the second part of the programme. Starting ten years ago, a huge effort was put into the production of a series of merchant classes, the majority being roll-on/roll-off (Ro-Ro) designs. By 1985 the Soviet navy will have at its disposal two 61,000-ton barge carriers (one nuclear-powered), two other barge carriers, two feeder barge carriers and three Ro-Flow ships (these five being similar in capability to the British *Fearless*-class assault ships), and over 50 Ro-Ro ships. The total carrying capacity of this large fleet, which is still expanding, is somewhere in the region of ten armoured divisions, or about half the British Army. There is no question of these ships being taken up from trade in the British manner. They are built from scratch with strengthened decks and large-volume exhaust systems, and have naval communications, Sigint and Elint aerials, photographic laboratories, tank hold-down facilities, nuclear, biological and chemical warfare protection and washdown facilities, replenishment equipment (in many cases), and a full range of self-repair equipment. Their steaming range varies from 3,000–10,000 miles for the smaller ships to 20,000–30,000 for the larger

Ivan Rogov, the first of a new class of dock landing ships, was completed at Kaliningrad in 1978. She was followed in 1982 by *Aleksandr Nikolayev* (shown here). These vessels represent a great advance on previous landing ships. They are larger, at 13,000 tons full load, faster at 25kt, carry four helicopters, are armed with a twin 76mm mounting, four Gatlings and a 122mm rocket launcher, and have a much increased carrying capacity. This includes a battalion of Naval Infantry and up to 20 tanks, and there is space in the dock for two Lebed-class hovercraft and an Ondatra LCM. The design of this class is now probably 20 years old and a new design may be expected in the near future.

The 17 Ropucha-class LSTs were completed in Poland between 1974 and 1983. Of 4,400 tons full load and with a speed of 18kt, they are about the same size as the earlier Alligator class but have an improved carrying capacity. (*US Navy*)

designs. Their complements invariably include both naval and military intelligence officers who are assisted in their duties by comprehensive navigational and cypher equipment. The fact that the Soviet Naval Infantry is only 18,000 strong should not be taken as a limiting factor on amphibious operations. Many army divisions are trained in landing techniques, and now they have the ships to transport them. These same vessels can be seen regularly in Western ports in their role as inoffensive merchant ships.

Aleksandr Tortsev is one of the six Alligator Type 3 LSTs. In all there are 14 of the class (Types 1–4). These 4,500-ton ships have operated in all parts of the world for nearly 20 years.

This drawing of one of two feeder barge carriers built by Valmet of Finland for the USSR's merchant fleet in 1982–84 shows the sort of "civilian" support that can be given to the Soviet amphibious forces when required. With an individual capacity of six 1,000-ton barges, these ships belong to a group of some 50 ostensibly civilian vessels built to accommodate troops, tanks and vehicles. They would form part of a naval amphibious force, lifting no fewer than ten divisions. (*Valmet*)

The Pauk class (illustrated) has the same hull as the Tarantul class but a very different armament. Pauk is an anti-submarine craft carrying a dipping sonar, four A/S torpedo tubes, two A/S rocket launchers and depth charges as well as a 76mm gun and a Gatling. Both classes have a full-load displacement of 500 tons but Tarantul is a gas-turbine craft and Pauk is diesel-driven. As a result, the former has a maximum speed of 36kt, the latter 32kt. The armament in Tarantul is four SS-N-2C or SS-N-22 anti-ship missiles, a 76mm gun and two Gatlings instead of one. Lead ships of the two classes appeared within a few months of each other in 1978–79.

This Natya I-class ocean minesweeper is one of a class of 34 ships of 765 tons full load. They are the largest ships in the Soviet mine countermeasures force of some 370 mine-sweepers and hunters. The Natyas, steel-hulled ships with a speed of 17kt, have frequently been deployed abroad.

Soviet second line marks time

Capt John Moore RN

The publication of an article on mine countermeasures (MCM) in the August 1984 *Soviet Military Review* combined with the emergence of the Red Sea mining affair to focus attention on this aspect of Russian naval activity. The article indicates that Soviet MCM does not differ markedly from Western practice. They have minehunting sonar, and photographs of underwater cameras suggest that television is a secondary method of search. The article also refers to the use of lasers for the purpose, though this is most unlikely in view of the high power requirements of such systems. Apart from normal wire, magnetic and acoustic sweeps, there is a surprising reference to "hydrodynamic sweeps" designed to detonate pressure mines. If such equipment exists, then Soviet scientists have certainly made

a great advance. But the claim should be treated with caution: the simulation of the changes in water pressure caused by a moving ship is a taxing problem that has so far defeated Western experts.

The huge Soviet MCM fleet consisted of 367 ships and craft at the last count, representing almost exactly a

The first Soviet intelligence-gathering ships appeared at the end of the 1950s. They were all built as or converted from trawler or other fishing vessel hulls. The original ten-ship force has now expanded to 64 vessels deployed worldwide, the latest being the 4,000-ton Balzam class, the first of which was completed in 1980. The photograph shows *Linza* of the Okean class, one of the older types. The escort is HMS *Brazen*. (H. W. van Boeijen)

▲ One of the tasks of the Soviet Pacific Fleet is the tracking of ▼ As the Soviet Navy extended its reach overseas in the 1960s it
missiles fired down the Pacific range. Six missile range ships
of the Desna (2) and *Sibir* (4) classes, all converted bulk ore
carriers, perform these duties. This photograph shows
Chumikan of the Desna class. The Ship Globe tracking radar
is set in the large dome above the bridge, while three tracking
directors are stacked forward. These two ships are the only
vessels in the Soviet Navy to carry Head Net B radars (two
Head Net A aerials back to back). The two horns above the
funnel are Vee Cone aerials for long-range HF communications.

began to feel a need for better fleet support than could be
provided by merchant ships backing up a comparative hand-
ful of fleet tankers. *Boris Chilikin*, lead ship of a class of six,
was completed in 1974, the remainder being commissioned
by 1978. This photograph of *Genrik Gasanov* clearly shows
the replenishment arrangements: liquids are supplied to port
forward and solids to starboard forward, and liquids from
both after positions and astern. The total load is 13,000 tons
of fuel and diesel, 400 tons of ammunition, 400 tons of victual-
ling stores and 500 tons of water.

As Soviet overseas deployments built up through the 1960s, the need for seagoing basic training facilities began to make itself felt. The first major move in this direction was the conversion of two of the Ugra-class submarine depot ships as training ships. Both *Borodin* and *Gangut* (shown here) were available for these duties by 1972. Of 7,500 tons full load, each carries 150 trainees. A new class, comprising *Smolny*, *Perekop* and *Khasan*, was completed in Poland in 1976–78; these ships carry 200 trainees in a 9,000-ton hull. All five are fully armed and available as warships in an emergency. The next five training ships, two Polish Wodnik-class carrying 150 trainees in an 1,800-ton hull and three elderly Mayak-class with 20 trainees, would be of little operational value and are probably employed on less extensive cruises than the larger ships. (*Selçuk Emre*)

third of the world total. It contains no new types, the most modern being the two ships of the *Andryusha* class, which are ten years old and probably experimental. It seems possible that in addition to rigging larger ships for MCM, the Soviet Navy may introduce a new class in the next few years.

Amongst the smaller ships and craft no new classes have appeared in the last year. The Nanuchka III class continues to be built at a slow rate, while the smaller Tarantul class is also in production, the first export model having been transferred to Poland in December 1983. The single Sarancha-class missile hydrofoil is almost certainly a research and development version, and Matka-class production seems to have ceased. The Pauk class, general-purpose FACs of 580 tons with a dipping sonar, are in series production to replace the Poti-class patrol craft. A number of new river patrol craft are also being built.

Although some of the activities of the KGB are now hazily understood in Western countries, the fact that the work of state security requires a sizeable fleet is less well known. Yet this maritime affiliation of the various Soviet secret forces goes back a long time. The naming of the KGB's eight Grisha II-class frigates after gemstones is an echo of the same usage by the Border Guard element of the NKVD in the 1930s.

These 950-ton ships, built in the 1970s, are the largest warships in a fleet of some 200 vessels. Some of the new Pauk-class FACs have been transferred to the KGB, joining the 95 members of the 210-ton Stenka-class patrol FACs and the 30 Zhuk-class 50-ton coastal patrol craft. Hydrofoils have figured in the KGB line-up ever since the 80-ton Pchela class was introduced in 1965, 20 craft in all being built. A new class of 250 tons, well armed and with a dipping sonar, is now under construction in the Black Sea. This addition of strictly naval equipment ensures that all KGB vessels could be handed over to the fleet in the event of an emergency of such severity that it overrode the clandestine service's priorities.

The same is true of the six Arctic patrol ships of the *Ivan Susanin* class, the heavily armed *Purga*, the dozen or so T-43-class minesweepers and the ten SO 1-class large patrol craft. There are also indications that the KGB operates several hovercraft, particularly in the Far East. All in all, this is a handy-sized fleet to ensure that Soviet citizens don't go visiting or, less likely, that foreigners don't drop into the USSR.

There has been little advance amongst the Soviet Navy's support and depot ships or in the service forces apart from an increase in the numbers of icebreakers and large tugs. The general impression is that the Soviet naval construction emphasis is now centred on submarines and major surface vessels.

A Soviet Navy Auxiliary exists in the form of the ships operated by the Border Guard of the Committee for State Security (KGB). This is a significant force, the largest warships being the eight vessels of the 1,200-ton Grisha II class of small frigates. Whereas Grisha I and III carry only one twin 57mm, the KGB variant has two twin mountings as well as a Gatling. All three types have four torpedo tubes and two RBU 6000 anti-submarine rocket launchers, but Grisha II does not carry the twin SA-N-4 launcher fitted in the others. (*US Navy*)

A number of Pauk-class 580-ton corvettes have been transferred to the KGB, as have all 95 Stenka-class 210-ton fast attack craft (patrol), shown here.